REDEEMER

REDEEMER

Who He Is and
Who He Will Always Be

DAVID BUTLER

DESERET
BOOK

Salt Lake City, Utah

Illustrations on pages 28, 40, 53, 69, 86, 103, 118, 130, 146, and 158 by Bernardo Ramonfaur. © Bernardo Ramonfaur/Shutterstock. Used by permission.

DESERET BOOK is a registered trademark of Deseret Book Company.

Visit us at deseretbook.com

Library of Congress Cataloging-in-Publication Data
(CIP on file)
ISBN 978-1-62972-574-1

Printed in the United States of America
Publishers Printing, Salt Lake City, UT

10 9 8 7 6 5 4 3

FOR SPENCEY—
who loves Jesus with all his heart
. . . but whom Jesus loves more.

INTRODUCTION

I used to think I didn't get starstruck very easily. You know those videos where celebrities surprise one of their fans at home, and the person is in the doorway covering his or her mouth in a muffled scream, too excited to breathe? I used to think, "Get control of yourself! It is just a person! Another human. My goodness!" Once I saw Mike Tyson in the Las Vegas airport. He was a super famous boxer back in the day. We passed each other in the terminal and I threw out an "Oh hey, Mike," and then kept walking. He shot back with a "What's up, buddy," and we both went our separate ways. No screaming. No hand over my mouth. No whispered "Oh my gosh, it's Mike Tyson." Just, "Hey, Mike." Then, "What's up, buddy." And that's it. Just how I like it.

Then I realized something. I've just never met the right person. I don't even like Mike Tyson that much. I had his video game on Nintendo and beat him every time. So of course it wasn't that big of a deal. But as I started thinking about it, I could easily and quickly make a list of people that even the possibility of ever meeting in real life makes my heart start to beat a little faster. I am fairly certain now that there are people that would cause me to scream like a little girl if I met them. I am getting sweaty palms thinking about it. I don't dare mention their names here, but I am going to write them down somewhere as future goals and try to will it into reality.

I have always wondered what my reaction and feeling will be like when I meet Jesus again. It won't be for the first time, but because of the veil, I don't remember it. So it might feel like it is.

WILL IT BE MELLOW,
or
WILL IT BE MAGNIFICENT?

WILL IT BE CASUAL,
or
WILL IT CAUSE MY HEART TO JUMP?

There is a dream story at the beginning of the Book of Mormon that symbolically plays out the scenario of meeting Jesus. (You're probably super familiar with it, but if not, you can read more about it in 1 Nephi 8.) The father-prophet Lehi had a vision he shared with his family one morning of a tree known as the tree of life. In the dream, there was a long, windy path that led to this spectacular tree. The path was crowded with people of every kind who were making their way toward the tree. As you would expect in any great story, it was a treacherous path. There was a gulf of filth- iness that some fell into, a mist of darkness that swallowed up some others, and what I've always pictured as a dazzling casino-like build- ing that was filled with people who laughed and mocked and lured away those who walked toward the tree. For those safety-first people out there, happily, there was also a firm, strong, and steady metal rod that travelers could cling to if they wanted to make it to the tree without falling into a gulf.

And those who did make it got the EXPERIENCE OF A LIFETIME—to eat the fruit from the tree. That does not sound like it is bucket list material at first, but this was not just any fruit you can pick up in the produce section of the grocery store. This was fruit that was described as the best of the best. PURE ABOVE ALL THAT IS PURE, DELICIOUS ABOVE ALL THAT IS DELICIOUS, PRECIOUS ABOVE ALL THAT WAS EVER PRECIOUS, and that had the power to fill a soul to overflowing with joy.[1] Strawberries probably come the closest, but this was fruit that represented a kind of feeling and experience that nothing else in this world can offer. Better than Hawaiian vacations, better than fat bank accounts, and better than a million billion followers on Instagram. It takes the gold medal every time. And if you made a pie out of it—game over.

The tree, we find out, represents Jesus. And the fruit represents those matchless and priceless gifts that come through and of and because of Him—gifts that He offers so willingly to any and all.

The story represents each of our individual journeys toward Him. Some of the folks in Lehi's dream, for whatever reason, never even start on the path to the tree, and there are others who leave or fall off along the way. But, interestingly, the group who makes it to the tree—those who hold tight to the rod, walk the path, and finally arrive—split into two separate groups. One group stays and relishes in the presence of the tree and devours the fruit in some sort of spectacular heavenly picnic. The other group gets there and tastes the fruit, and then, hearing the mocking yells from the building, in eat-and-run style, they leave in shame. I have always been so puzzled by that second group. HOW COULD THEY WALK AWAY?? AND WHAT MADE THE FIRST GROUP WANT TO STAY? WHAT IS THE DIFFERENCE BETWEEN THESE FOLKS?

One day while reading the dream again, I noticed something

I hadn't before. Here is a side-by-side comparison of those two groups. I want you to picture it in your mind (remember it is a vision, so it is meant to be seen). Play it out like a movie in your head and see what you notice about the difference between the two.

▶ ━━━━━━━━━━━━━━━━━━━━━━━━━━━━━━━━

THOSE WHO LEAVE:

"They did press forward through the mist of darkness, clinging to the rod of iron, even until they did come forth and partake of the fruit of the tree. And after they had partaken of the fruit of the tree they did cast their eyes about as if they were ashamed" (1 Nephi 8:24–25).

THOSE WHO STAY:

"They did press their way forward, continually holding fast to the rod of iron, until they came forth and fell down and partook of the fruit of the tree. . . . And great was the multitude that did enter into that strange building. And after they did enter into that building they did point the finger of scorn at me and those that were partaking of the fruit also; but we heeded them not" (1 Nephi 8:30, 33).

I am sure there are several differences between these groups that we could learn from, but the thing that popped off the page for me when I read it was the way they arrived at the tree. Did you catch it? The second group "FELL DOWN" when they got there. Normally, you reach up when you get to a tree—to pick the fruit—but this group fell down. WHY? WHY WOULD THEY RESPOND THAT WAY? The imagery gets better when you remember what the tree symbolizes.

It is Jesus.

The group who stayed fell down at the feet of Jesus.

Have you ever fallen down when you have met someone? I have had some happy, happy reunions in my life, but not once, no, never, have I had one that has made my knees buckle and give out. I am a mama's boy, and I didn't even do that when I first saw my mom after my mission. When I pass through the Salt Lake City airport and see a family waiting for their returning missionary, I always wait and watch. I am so into it. I can't help it. And yes, I cry every time when I see the missionaries hug their mom. Once I even hugged the missionary, who was a complete stranger, because I got so caught up in the moment. But in all those times, I have never seen someone fall. So why does that happen to the people in the dream?

What feelings or thoughts were stirring in their hearts that caused them to fall down at His feet?

On the outside, these two groups looked almost identical. They both held on to the rod, which symbolizes God's word, and were obedient and did not leave the gospel path. They were church-going, commandment-keeping, scripture-reading people. All of them. It seems like you could visit any Sunday School class or sacrament meeting and not be able to tell the difference between these two groups. Both on the path. Both holding on. Not swimming in the gulf.

However, something significantly different was happening on the inside.

So I asked myself the important question.

WHICH GROUP AT THE TREE WOULD I BE A PART OF?

What would my reaction actually be—or *will* it actually be, I should say—when I meet Jesus again?

Maybe there is a way I can know before I meet Him. My friend was at the pulpit one Sunday telling a story about a trip she took to Disneyland about a month after her mission. She was waiting in line (of course!), and as she stood there, munching on one of those expensive, fancy churros with all the cinnamon glittering to the ground, she overheard the name of someone she knew in someone else's conversation somewhere in the back of the line.

The name of Jesus.

Her heart bounced in her chest and she whipped around with excitement, looking in the direction it came from. Just as she was about to call out to the people who were talking, she stopped her words when she realized it could have been a tiny bit socially awkward to yell out "I KNOW HiM!" about Jesus in a crowded line somewhere in Tomorrowland. Even though she never had that conversation with the strangers, she realized something about herself that warmed her heart more than anything the happiest place on earth could offer.

SHE HAD A FRIEND IN JESUS.

Somehow over the previous years, she had developed a meaningful, authentic admiration and adoration of Him. The very mention of His name instinctively lit off fireworks in her soul. That unexpected reaction had revealed what a treasure He had become to her. She didn't just know *about* Him—she realized that she knew Him and loved Him in a way that would cause her to fall at His feet.

I sat there in wonder as I listened. I asked myself, "Is that me? Does my heart leap at the mention of His name? Do I love Him with that same fervor?" I wanted to. I wanted to think of Him and love Him as deeply as she seemed to. I wanted to be in the fall-down group—a man filled with gratitude, admiration, adoration, honor, and love. To be excited not because I was supposed to be, but because I just was. That was my wish.

I left that morning meeting on a quest. A quest that has brought me here, and one that I am inviting you on, too.

IT IS A QUEST
to begin to come to know
Jesus Christ.

All about Him. A quest to find out more about who He is and what He does that makes some people turn with excitement when they hear His name or makes them run to Him and fall down at His feet. It feels exciting to begin this, doesn't it? It stirs my heart in a different way than those names on my "can't-wait-to-meet" list. More wonder than wow. More awestruck than starstruck. Not a hand-over-my-mouth muffled scream but a hand-over-my-heart moment of sacredness. I'm drawn to know Him from somewhere deep in me—and I want to know why. I can just sense this is going to be good.

WHAT'S IN A NAME?

All lifelong friendships begin with an introduction. And all introductions, if you're normal, usually start with a name. One of my favorite friends in the world is named Daisy. He is a boy. Yep, a boy named Daisy. I wish I could see your facial expression right now. I had the same one. So does everyone who meets him. It usually goes like this:

"Hi, WHAT'S YOUR NAME?"
"DAiSY."
"DAVEY?"
"No. DAiSY."
"DAiSY?"
"YESSiR."
"HOW DO YOU SPELL iT?"
"D-A-I-S-Y. LiKE THE FLOWER."
"REALLY?"
"REALLY, REALLY."
"OKAY. UH, COOL NAME, MAN."
"THANK YOU."

Ha ha. I love watching it happen.

Once we went to the rec center to play racquetball and met an older guy who wanted to play with us. We went around the circle introducing ourselves, and when we got to Daisy and he said his name, the man actually reached to turn up his hearing aids before he said, "Oh, I'm sorry, I mix up my consonants and vowels. I thought you said Daisy. What is it again?" It was classic.

Daisy isn't the name that everyone knows him by. Like a lot of names, there is a story behind why people call him that. Knowing the story has made the name, and him, more endearing to those who know him. It makes you like him even more. When you hear Daisy, you might think, "Weird name." When I hear Daisy, I think of everything that it means, and everything that he is, and it makes me smile.

This happens with the names of Jesus. When you first hear them, they might not mean much to you. You might even think, "Weird name." But as you get to know what each name means, it becomes a name that makes you smile.

WE CAN LEARN A LOT ABOUT WHO JESUS IS BY WHAT HIS FRIENDS CALLED HIM.

John the Baptist was a dear friend of Jesus. For months and months John had been meeting with folks down by the river and had been teaching them and promising them that one day he would introduce them to his friend—someone so good and so amazing, by the way, that John didn't even feel worthy to kneel down and buckle up the friend's sandals. And then one day, He came. I picture John sitting by the water, wearing his camel-skin clothes, munching on crickets, preaching the good word, when he looked up and saw Jesus coming up over the crest of the hill. His heart must have skipped a beat, and with some excitement bubbling over, maybe he lifted his hand to point in Jesus's direction as he said to those near him:

"BEHOLD THE LAMB OF GOD!"
(John 1:36).

The Lamb of God? Like a sheep? Why do you think John the Baptist chose that name for his introduction of Jesus Christ?

Whatever the reason (a reason we will talk about later), it won over at least two of the listeners and they started following Jesus. They were intrigued. They wanted to know more. You can read this whole story I am about to retell in John chapter 1.

Jesus turned back to look at the men walking behind Him and asked them what they wanted.

"WHAT SEEK YE?"
Jesus asked them.

"Where dwellest thou?" they answered.

Uh, where do you live? Kind of a funny question to ask when you first meet someone. I generally don't ask for people's addresses on day one. Maybe these men were a little starstruck, or maybe it was a way of asking what they really wanted to know.

WE WANT TO KNOW WHAT YOU ARE ALL ABOUT.
WHO ARE YOU?
WHAT DO YOU DO?
AND WHAT DOES JOHN KNOW ABOUT YOU THAT WE DON'T?

The Savior responded with a simple invitation:

"Come and see."

And so they did. And you know what? They ended up staying all day! (And in case you don't end up reading the whole Bible—they end up staying their whole lives as friends and followers of Jesus!)

One of those men was Andrew. After his day with Jesus, he ran looking for his brother Simon. He had to take him to Jesus.

"WE HAVE FOUND THE MESSIAS," he told him (v. 41). A name that means "promised deliverance."

Simon was immediately intrigued, abandoned his plans for the day, and followed his brother to Jesus. We will talk more about their conversation later, but it ended with Simon and Andrew going to get their buddy Philip.

Then Philip went looking right away for his best guy Nathanael. He had to meet Him too!

Philip found Nathanael and told him he had met THE ONE PROPHESIED ABOUT IN THE SCRIPTURES. Jesus of Nazareth.

Nathanael was shocked and maybe chuckled a bit. Jesus? Nazareth? Back then, the name Jesus was really common. Like Jim. And Nazareth was not the holy city! It was a poor village off the beaten path. Like some small town in North Dakota. No road went through Nazareth. Nobody ever went on vacation there. It was the sticks! Certainly "the prophesied one" couldn't be from Nazareth! Nothing good came from Nazareth!

HOW COULD THIS COMMON-NAMED MAN FROM A BACKWOODS CITY BE ANYTHING SPECIAL?

But Philip didn't fight back. These things can't be forced. *I get it, I get it*, he must have thought. But then he just gave the same invitation: "Come and see" (v. 46).

↓ ↓ ↓ ↓ ↓

Come find out for yourself.
Come meet Him.

So he did. And he got more than he bargained for. That's usually the case with Jesus.

When Jesus saw Nathanael coming, He called out to him before there was a chance for proper introductions.

"Behold an Israelite indeed, in whom is no guile!" (v. 47).

Here is a man with a heart of gold. A pure soul. A ten out of ten. Nathanael must have melted.

He had never met Jesus, and yet the first words he heard from Him were heart-stopping.

How do you know me? he asked.

They had never met or been introduced. Jesus didn't even know his name. How could He know his heart?

Jesus answered, perhaps with an intriguing smile typical of His nature, "Before . . . Philip called thee, when thou wast under the fig tree, I saw thee" (v. 48).

And then listen to Nathanael's response:

"Thou art the Son of God; thou art the King of Israel."

Now that was a little over the top, don't you think? Nathanael asked how Jesus knew him, and Jesus answered by saying He saw him under the fig tree. That's it. Nothing more. A typical response to someone seeing you under a tree would probably be, "Oh, okay. Neat."

But Nathanael went all in. Jesus told him He saw him under a tree, and Nathanael fell down in worship!

There must have been more to the fig tree comment that we don't know. Something significant must have happened to get a response like that. We wish we knew what it was! But whatever it was, it won over Nathanael and he quickly knew that Jesus was more than just a street preacher.

I love what Jesus said to Nathanael next: "Because I said unto thee, I saw thee under the fig tree, believest thou?" (v. 50).

"That's why you believe?" Jesus essentially said to Nathanael. "That's all it took??"

Then comes this line—this promise—to Nathanael and me and you:

"THOU SHALT SEE GREATER THINGS THAN THESE"
(V. 50).

Oh, Nathanael . . . buckle up! This is only the beginning!

And that is the start of the story of lifelong friendships between Jesus and some of His disciples. FIRST BYSTANDERS, AND THEN BELIEVERS, AND THEN BURSTING WITH GREATER THINGS.

Something I like about this story is how after meeting Jesus, each of these disciples wanted to introduce Him to someone else. You know when you see a good movie or a funny YouTube video or meme and you have to pass it on? In a higher and holier yet just as exciting way, Jesus went viral before it was even a thing. After an authentic encounter with Jesus, they were in. Hooked! This is a pattern with people who come into contact with Jesus. First they are introduced, then they learn a little more about Him, and then they spend their lives with Him.

Jesus once said, "Learn of me, and listen to my words; walk in the meekness of my Spirit, and you shall have peace in me" (D&C 19:23). Check out the order of that.

First, we learn of Him.
Then we listen to His voice.
And then, we walk with Him.

Once we know who He is, then we want to hear what He has to say. And then, once we hear what He says to us and about us, *then* we will want to walk with Him. This is what happened to all of the disciples in the story. THEY WEREN'T DISCIPLES IN THE BEGINNING—ALL THEY STARTED WITH WAS HIS NAME.

Did you notice that each of those early disciples used a different name to describe the person he was waiting for? These names must have meant something to them. John the Baptist saw the Lamb of God. Peter was watching for a Messiah. Philip told Nathanael that the "one prophesied about" had come. And Nathanael finally praised Him as the "King of Israel." Why did they each choose these different names? What did each one mean to them? And what do they teach us about Him?

Throughout scripture, Jesus is given well over a hundred unique names. Each name has a story and meaning. One of my favorite names is *Redeemer*. The title *Redeemer* comes from a Hebrew word that means someone who will rescue or save by any means. He finds a way. Whatever it takes. By any means. Sometimes that is as the Shepherd, and other times as a Lamb. On this day as an Advocate, and on that one as the King. Throughout this book, we are going to look at some of these names as a way to learn a little bit more about who He is, what He does, the means by which He saves, and most importantly, what He feels about you.

I hope that learning who He is leads us to want to learn more. To listen to His words. To follow Him close behind. And in the end, I hope we praise the way Nephi did at the end of his life when he said,

> "I glory in plainness; I glory in truth; I glory in
> # MY JESUS,
> for he hath redeemed my soul from hell"
> (2 Nephi 33:6).

I love his praising soul! "My Jesus." Not just Jesus, or this Jesus, but *my* Jesus. Someone Nephi claimed as his own. That sounds like someone who knows something about Him. Someone who has met Him, heard His words, felt rescued and loved by Him, found Him completely irresistible, and eventually decided to follow Him, walking side by side, in a lifelong relationship.

So COME AND SEE—AND THEN HOPEFULLY STAY ALL DAY. Come learn a little more about Him—the Lamb of God, the Mighty Jehovah, the Loyal Advocate, the Anticipated King, Jesus Christ.

I wonder which name you will end up loving the most. Which one will make your heart bounce? Which one will endear Him to you?

And when you pass on the good news to someone else, which name will you use to introduce Him?

THE MIGHTY JEHOVAH

When I was younger, I brought my brother to the top of the stairs to have him witness something amazing. There I was, with goggles on my face, a green towel tucked into the back of my shirt as a cape, and a promise that he was about to watch me fly. I had seen it on TV, and it did not look that hard. I counted down from three. I got to about one and a half when I started to wonder if this was really such a good idea. Maybe it needed to be a red cape. But before I could bail on the plan, I heard a voice that wasn't mine yell "Go!" and got a little helpful push from behind. I didn't fly. That night ended with disappointment and a trip to the hospital. But what did not end was my fascination with superheroes or magic or the out-of-the-world stuff you usually only find in books or movies. It only takes one Halloween night to look around and see that this wasn't just a "me" thing. People are into the amazing. We all seem to yearn for some sort of strength or ability or power or person that is beyond what seems possible.

Maybe this is why I have always loved the OLD TESTAMENT. That is a book that has pages filled with iMPOSSiBLE STORIES. Man-eating whales, talking donkeys, city walls falling by blowing trumpets, and the bones of a dead man bringing someone else back to life. J. K. Rowling and Marvel have got nothing on the Old Testament. Some of the stories seem like they belong in fairy tales—legends from another realm, not our world. Believe it or not, though, they did happen in our world. And they are true! Looks like you don't need a train to Hogwarts or a meeting with the Avengers to experience the magnificent after all.

I think one of the reasons we are so drawn to heroes and magic is because that is exactly what we need sometimes.

EVERY NOW AND THEN (OR MAYBE MORE OFTEN THAN THAT), THIS WORLD DISHES UP IMPOSSIBLE SITUATIONS THAT NEED IMPOSSIBLE SOLUTIONS.

It's always been like that. Do you remember when Moses talked with the Lord in a burning bush? (Another wild story!) In Exodus 3, we find out that Moses was a regular shepherd and one day was taking his ordinary flock of sheep up the typical mountain to graze when he turned and noticed a bush that seemed to be on fire. And then out of the bush, the voice of God called Moses to the impossible task of going back to Egypt to tell the pharaoh to let all of the children of Israel go free. You have to remember the story to know why this was such a tall task. Moses was a runaway from Egypt. He was considered a fugitive there. How could he go back? And the whole economy of Egypt was built on the backs of slaves—the Israelites. If Pharaoh let them go free, it would bankrupt the country. There was no way Moses could go back, and there was no way that Pharaoh would let them go. Not in a million years. But that is what God was asking.

And He is capable of performing one-in-a-million kind of miracles.

While they were talking, Moses expressed his well thought-out worries and concerns. How out of this world it seemed. Pharaoh, the royal guards, even the children of Israel—they would never believe him. What would he say? "A bush told me to come lead you out of Egypt"?

"Who am I," he said to the Lord, "that I should go unto Pharaoh, and that I should bring forth the children of Israel out of Egypt?" (Exodus 3:11).

It seems like Moses responded the way a lot of us would—saying something like, "Sorry, but I think you've got the wrong guy. And I'm not sure if you know this, but Egypt is big and their army is big, and I know Pharaoh, and there is no way he will let them go."

But then the Lord says, "CERTAINLY I WILL BE WITH THEE; . . . and this shall be a token unto thee, that I have sent thee: . . . thus shalt thou say unto the children of Israel, I AM hath sent me unto you. . . . the LORD GOD of your fathers, the God of Abraham, the God of Isaac, and the God of Jacob, hath sent me" (vv. 12, 14–15).

Moses asked "Who am I?" and God responded by gently reminding him that it didn't matter, because "I AM."

The phrase "I AM" is actually a name of Jesus Christ.

When it is translated into Hebrew it is pronounced Yahweh, or in the more common English spelling, Jehovah. Before He was born in Bethlehem, Jesus was Lord God of the universe. The God you read about in Old Testament stories and much of the Book of Mormon is Jesus Christ before He came to the world. The name He was known by before He was born is Jehovah. In the King James Bible, the name *Jehovah* is usually translated and shows up as LORD with capital letters. Sometimes as we read the scriptures, we wonder if the phrase LORD or God is talking about Jesus Christ or Heavenly Father. The two of them are so alike and are working together so closely that it really it doesn't matter. Except for a few instances, when you say something about one of Them, you are saying it about both of Them.

The neat thing about the word *Jehovah* in Hebrew is that it is both a name and a sentence. The translation, a short two-word sentence, I AM, can be translated as the past, present, and future tense of that sentence—I was, I am, and I will be.

> THE NAME JEHOVAH MEANS THAT WHO HE WAS IN THE PAST IS WHO HE IS TODAY, AND WHO HE IS TODAY IS WHO HE WILL ALWAYS BE.

The children of Israel had grown up on stories of the LORD, or Jehovah. Before their good-night kisses at bedtime, Israelite mamas told their babies stories of Adam and Eve, Enoch, Noah, Abraham, Isaac, and Jacob, and the amazing things Jehovah, the LORD, had done for them. It is a name associated with MIRACLES, STRENGTH, AND POWER. When Moses used His name, he was reminding the children of Israel that the miraculous God of those bedtime stories was the same God who would be there for them when they needed Him. If they were ever scared, nervous, or worried, they could REMEMBER that name and remember that the God of Abraham, Isaac, and Jacob was there—the mighty Jehovah—the Great I AM.

Maybe this name gave Moses courage for what he was being asked to do too.

Can you imagine what the experience was like for Moses and the Israelites in Egypt?

After ten plagues had swept through the land—the frogs and flies and locusts and all of it (all Jehovah's handiwork, by the way)— Pharaoh had finally decided to let the Israelites go. They had lived as slaves their entire lives, and now they were free. A miracle!

But the miracles were not over
(and spoiler alert—they never will be).

As they left the city and traveled a short distance into the desert, they came face-to-face with an ocean that stretched as far as they could see (you can read more of this story for yourself in amazing detail in Exodus 14). This was only a minor problem until all of a sudden the Egyptian army shows up over the horizon behind them. They were one of the largest and most dangerous armies of the ancient world and were coming at them full speed. All of Pharaoh's chariots. All of his horses. All of his soldiers. And no doubt, they all had sharp things in their hands.

With sand to their left and sand to their right, an army behind them and an ocean in front of them, the Israelites were doomed. Dead meat. Trapped! What would they do? There seemed to be no other option besides death. This was an impossible situation. All eyes turned to Moses.

We have no idea how or what he was possibly feeling, but these are the words the LORD Jehovah put into his heart:

"FEAR YE NOT, STAND STILL, AND SEE THE SALVATION OF THE LORD, WHICH HE WILL SHEW TO YOU TO DAY.... THE LORD SHALL FIGHT FOR YOU.... GO FORWARD.... AND THE EGYPTIANS SHALL KNOW THAT I AM THE LORD"

(Exodus 14:13–15, 18).

That line pumps me up! Whoo! Then, after that mighty declaration from Jehovah, in a way that had never happened before, the Red Sea opened right up like a storybook. Just like that, the word *impossible* was erased from the Israelites' vocabulary. I hope there is a big movie in the sky after we die, because I cannot wait to see the look on everyone's faces when that ocean split in two.

And, P.S., every time you read or talk about the Red Sea story, make sure you don't miss the DOUBLE MIRACLE that happened. The ocean opened, yes, but "the children of Israel went into the midst of the sea upon the DRY GROUND" (Exodus 14:22). Miracle number one was that the ocean opened. But not only did the sea open up; the ground they walked on was dry—ground that had been saturated under the water for centuries was now dry enough to walk on. Not goopy thick mud, but dry as a bone. That was miracle number two. Don't you love that?

When the Lord performs a miracle, He never performs it halfway.

There isn't anything He hasn't thought of, and there isn't anything He cannot do. He will get you to your promised land even if it takes a thousand miracles (and it probably will).

JESUS CHRIST IS A GOD OF MIGHTY MIRACLES. HE WAS AND IS THE MIGHTY JEHOVAH, THE GREAT I AM.

He can do anything, anytime, anywhere—back then and now. That is what that name teaches us. It reminds us that He is so big and so mighty, there is nothing our God cannot do. You can read this over and over and over again in the scriptures. Do you remember that day when the prophet Elisha was with his servant in a mountain cave surrounded by an enemy army? (see 2 Kings 6:12–19 for the story). They were trapped and outnumbered, just like Moses's people had been. "Alas, my master!" the little servant boy said. "How shall we do?" (I love how that is translated. We need to use the word *alas* more often—don't you think?) And then Elisha asked the LORD to open the servant's eyes so he could see what was really going on in those hills. And he saw! The mountainside was flooded with angel armies.

"FEAR NOT," ELISHA SAID, "FOR THEY THAT BE WITH US ARE MORE THAN THEY THAT BE WITH THEM."

If he had wanted to, Elisha could've said that line a little differently and it would have still been true. Maybe something like this: "Fear not. For HE that be with us is more than any of them."

THE LORD'S STRENGTH IS BIG ENOUGH TO SOLVE THE PROBLEM. HIS HEART IS BIG ENOUGH TO BE WILLING.

Think of all of the miracles found in the scriptures.
What are your favorites?

_____

_____

_____

_____

They were all performed by Him. He created the world, He fought Joshua's battles, He was with David when he conquered Goliath, He tamed Daniel's lions, and He saved Esther from the king. He knocked down the prison walls that held Alma and Amulek, He defended Ammon as he disarmed the Lamanites, and He shielded Samuel from all those arrows and stones. He is the mighty Jehovah of the Old Testament and is also the Jesus of great miracles in the New. He healed the lepers, gave sight to the blind, and raised the dead.

Again and again and again.

And who He was, is who He will always be. His miracles have not ceased (see Moroni 7:35–37).

I figured that out for myself a few years ago while I was visiting the Holy Land on a trip with my mom. It was a dream trip, and I think you should all add it to your bucket list right this second. During our travels, we visited the area near the SEA OF GALILEE. This is the place where most of Jesus's STORIES AND MIRACLES that we love from the New Testament happened. One day as we traveled around the cities near Nazareth, I started to get a stomachache. It started out annoying, but by the middle of the night it was excruciating! I felt like someone was stabbing me over and over in the stomach. I had never been in so much physical pain. I wanted to die!

As nervous as I was, being in an unfamiliar country, I finally decided I should probably go to the hospital. On my dream trip! Lame! Before we left in a taxi to head to Jerusalem, I called some of my new friends I had met on the trip and asked if they would come and give me a priesthood blessing. One of my friends who was there had just been ordained an elder and had received the Melchizedek Priesthood right before he came on the trip. I asked him if he would give me the blessing. He had never given a blessing before, and I thought it would be neat if He gave His first one on the shores of the Galilee.

As he laid his hands on my head, I started to think about how unique this experience actually was. Centuries before, somewhere near that little cabin I was staying in, THE LORD HAD LAID HANDS ON THE SICK IN THAT VERY PLACE! As my friend spoke the words of the blessing, I could hear the waves of the sea outside my window.

The same sea that He had walked on. The same sea that He had created. The same sea that He had calmed when it got wild.

My friend held the holy priesthood—the authority to speak blessings and miracles in the name of Jesus Christ, the mighty Jehovah.

After my blessing, I took a bumpy ride to the hospital, got emergency surgery, and spent seven glorious days in a Middle Eastern hospital. I found out later that I had been in bigger trouble than I had originally thought. Apparently, when I got out of surgery, I slept for two days straight, and a few of the doctors and nurses told me afterward that during those forty-eight hours they didn't think I was going to live. I suppose under normal circumstances someone could say it was an impossible recovery. Impossible without Jehovah, the God of miracles, that is. He was a God of miracles in the past, and in that place, He performed another miracle for me in the present. Priesthood holders pronounced that miracle upon me in His holy name.

BECAUSE OF HIM, BLIND PEOPLE SEE. BECAUSE OF HIM, DEAF PEOPLE HEAR. BECAUSE OF HIM, THOSE WHO TOOK THEIR LAST BREATH BREATHE AGAIN. HE OPENED OCEANS IN THE PAST, AND HE STILL DOES TODAY.

He is the mighty Jehovah, and He can and will and does perform miracles as amazing as those witnessed in the scriptures. Miracles just as powerful as the ones we read about in Genesis, Exodus, Matthew, Mark, Luke, and Alma. They are recorded in the journals, memories, and hearts of people all over the world. For He is "the same yesterday, and to day, and for ever" (Hebrews 13:8).

It is important to remember that even though Jesus can perform the miracles we want, He sometimes chooses not to. There were miracles He didn't perform in the past, and there are miracles He holds back on today as well. Do you remember the story of Lazarus? When He was deathly ill, his sisters sent messengers to Jesus begging Him to come heal their brother. Lazarus was one of Jesus's best friends. But do you know what He did when He got the message? The scriptures say He stayed where He was for another two days (see John 11:6). Two days! One of his best guys was in an emergency situation, and Jesus decides to just hold back. What was He doing? We don't know. But the point is, He did, and His friend died.

HE KNOWS WHEN, WHY, AND WHERE HE SHOULD INTERVENE IN OUR STORIES. HIS PERSPECTIVE IS ETERNAL.

One day, He will be able to share with us why He held back. Perhaps, we will learn the "why" while we are still living here on the earth, or maybe it won't come until after we have left. But whenever it is, we need time and His perspective to be able to understand. And when we eventually understand, we will thank Him for whatever He did.

He doesn't just know what is good for us, He knows what is best for us—and that is what He always does.

He is the God of miracles. He has a miracle for you, but it might not be the one you were expecting or come when you were expecting it. Just because He doesn't perform a miracle the way you pray for doesn't mean He can't, and it certainly doesn't mean that He doesn't care.

Perhaps we can learn from Nephi in situations like that. Once upon a time, the Lord asked Nephi to build a boat to cross an ocean. Nephi wasn't sure what the Lord had in mind. He was taking it day by day. When his brothers complained, called him foolish, and told him it was impossible, he reminded them (and maybe himself) about the great miracles God had performed in the past. You can read them all in 1 Nephi 17:1–50, but this is his conclusion at the end:

"If God had commanded me to do all things I could do them. If he should command me that I should say unto this water, be thou earth, it should be earth; and if I should say it, it would be done. And now, if the Lord has such great power, and has wrought so many miracles among the children of men, how is it that he cannot instruct me, that I should build a ship?" (1 Nephi 17:50–51).

REMEMBERING WHO GOD HAD BEEN IN THE PAST GAVE NEPHI COURAGE TO TRUST HIM IN THE PRESENT.

Throughout our lives, you and I might witness or need miracles just as unbelievable as the one Moses saw at the Red Sea. Perhaps our lives will be FILLED with a mountain-load of LITTLE MIRACLES instead—a text that comes right when you needed it, remembering an answer on a test, or finding your keys after a prayer. Whatever those miracles look like, big or small, you should know that all of His miracles are performed by Him as acts of love.

HIS GREATEST MIRACLE OF ALL SHOWED
THE GREATEST AMOUNT OF LOVE—NOT THE DAY HE OPENED
THE RED SEA TO SAVE THE SLAVES, BUT THE DAY
HE OPENED THE DOOR TO HEAVEN AND DELIVERED US
FROM THE SLAVERY OF SIN AND DEATH.

We will talk about that miracle more later on—a miracle we all will experience someday.

For those moments when you are on the shores of your own Red Sea, or in the mountains surrounded by armies, or sick by the sea-shore, or asked to build a ship, I hope you will remember you have Jehovah near you. He exists, and He is mighty to save. He is a God who is both willing and able to do amazing things for those He loves. A God who will split seas. A God who will heal. He is the Great I AM. And He is who He will always be.

THE MIGHTY JEHOVAH

Is all-knowing and all-powerful.
Performs breathtaking miracles for you.
Can do anything, anytime, anywhere.

2

THE WATCHFUL SHEPHERD

When my oldest boys were little, I took them to an amusement park because I'm such a rocking dad. During lunch, while we were all standing in line for a million-dollar hamburger, I looked down to where my son Jack had been standing right next to me. He wasn't there. I kind of leaned and bopped and spun my head around for a minute to spot him somewhere behind someone's legs, but I couldn't see him anywhere in the crowd. I was sort of bugged to lose my spot in line, but I figured he had wandered back to the rest of our crew who were saving a table, so I left the line to check at the table only to find them Jack-less. No sign of him. And no one had seen him. I started to worry a little. I stayed cool for about six seconds as we started to spread out around the restaurant, but worry quickly escalated to panic. I have lost keys and wallets, but never a full human before. I kept thinking about worst-case scenarios, and I started moving faster and more forcefully through the crowded restaurant. I yelled out his name again and again like a maniac while I prayed in my heart and looked frantically for my lost little boy. People started to notice. I started to wonder when it was normal to call the police. Looking back, I don't think it was that long, but in that moment each second felt like an hour. I was flustered and afraid out of my mind. Finally, I spotted him through a window! He had left the restaurant and was about fifty yards away in a gift shop having a little toddler conversation with a stuffed robot car. I cannot tell you the explosion of emotion I had. Gratitude he was found. Anger that he had wandered off. Stupidity for losing him. And a little bit of relief when I remembered that Mary and Joseph lost Jesus once. For three days. I didn't feel as bad. The whole range of emotions surged through my veins, and my eyes watered with tears of every kind. Then, in what might be the worst parenting move of this century, I decided to go grab him from behind, cover his mouth, and run off in a fake kidnapping attempt so he would learn his lesson on why I had told him not to run off in the first place. I kind of forgot the fact that no one else in the park knew it was a fake kidnapping and that I was his dad. Yep. That didn't go over super well.

Truthfully, I had no right to be that mad at Jack for wandering off. It is in his DNA, and he did not get it from his mother. I am a wanderer. It is actually in all of our DNA.

We are all prone to wander.

We are all seconds away from getting lost. We are also prone to falling, failing, and forgetting. It's kind of what we do best. This is probably one of the reasons why the scriptures compare us to sheep more than three hundred times!

Being compared to a sheep is not exactly a compliment. I don't think the Lord is trying to put us down, but sheep are not the smartest of creatures in the animal kingdom. I've never raised sheep before (except for those three days I babysat a lamb named Becky), but I have had several friends who have, and apparently, raising them can be a major pain in the rear. Let's start with the fact that my farming friends tell me SHEEP ARE DIRECTIONLESS. Like Jack and I, they are wanderers and followers, easily get lost, and don't know how to find their way back home. Or they get distracted and forget they even have a home. THEY ARE BOTH NEEDY AND ABSENTMINDED. All they do is eat, move, sleep, and eat, move, sleep. And sometimes they *baaa*. THEY ARE NEVER SATISFIED AND DO NOT KNOW WHAT THEY WANT. That's precisely why they are famous for walking off, following anything, and getting lost. I have a friend who lost his whole flock of sheep once because one of them found a hole in the fence and the rest of them just followed her out. Luckily there wasn't a cliff nearby, because they are dumb enough to follow a fellow sheep off of one of those, too. Bless their cotton-ball hearts.

Sheep are also completely defenseless.

Such an easy target for predators. They are not very agile, are not quick on their hooves, and wool is not exactly great armor. If I were a wolf, I would totally go after sheep. Squirrels are too speedy, and porcupines are walking weapons. Sheep are like a wolf drive-thru. Fast, cheap, and easy.

And oh, you will die at this! Because of their body shape, sheep can also become cast. Cast means they tip upside down and are not able to flip back over onto their feet on their own. It makes me want to laugh but mostly cry to think of a sheep just out in a field some-where, upside down, wiggling its feet in the air, unable to flip back over. Just picture it!

You don't have to talk to someone who has raised sheep very long to learn how HIGH-MAINTENANCE these fluffy little farm animals are! They consistently NEED PROTECTION, DIRECTION, HEALING, FEEDING, AND REST. They are an investment—not only to buy them, but also every day you are in charge of them. CONSTANT CARE IS REQUIRED. 24/7.

They just cannot make it on their own. Just like us.

"All we like sheep have gone astray," Isaiah said. "We have turned every one to his own way" (Isaiah 53:6). Isaiah was right—we are all like sheep. Needy little sheep. We are defenseless and high-maintenance; we wander and get caught in situations upside down just like sheep do.

HAPPILY, WE ARE NOT ONLY NEEDY SHEEP BUT ALSO LUCKY SHEEP. BECAUSE WE HAVE A SHEPHERD. AND NOT JUST ANY SHEPHERD, BUT THE GOOD SHEPHERD. THE BEST SHEPHERD.

This is one of the names of Jesus—a name that shows us how He can and does care for each of the individual wants, needs, hopes, and dreams of us, His sheep.

"Wherefore, I am in your midst, and I am the good shepherd" (D&C 50:44).

"Fear not, little flock" (Luke 12:32).

King David knew this well. He was one of the great and mighty kings of the Bible. But before the palace life, he grew up in the Bethlehem fields as a shepherd. He knew the drill all too well—the leading, the watching over, the caring. When he was older, he wrote a famous song that is in the book of Psalms. It is about a shepherd. From all of his experience, David knew that he was like a sheep, and the name he thought fit best for Jesus was "the Shepherd." His shepherd.

> "The Lord is my shepherd; I shall not want.
>
> He maketh me to lie down in green pastures: he leadeth me
>   beside the still waters.
>
> He restoreth my soul. . . .
>
> Yea, though I walk through the valley of the shadow of death,
>   I will fear no evil: for thou art with me;
>
> Thy rod and thy staff they comfort me. . . .
>
> Thou anointest my head with oil; my cup runneth over.
>
> Surely goodness and mercy shall follow me all the days of my life."
>
> (Psalm 23)

Don't you love that psalm? Look at what it teaches about Jesus as a shepherd:

"THE LORD IS MY SHEPHERD; I SHALL NOT WANT." Sheep are always looking for something else to eat or drink. They never seem satisfied—always wanting something more and moving from place to place to get it. We are the same way, aren't we? We are always moving on to the next best thing. We can never quite have enough! When the iPhone 20 comes out, we will be waiting for the 21.

BUT JESUS, AS OUR SHEPHERD, CAN SATISFY OUR SOULS.

He knows what we truly need. He is what we truly need. Jesus once met a woman by the side of a well. You can read this story in John 4:7–29. She was there drawing water for herself or her family. As she dipped her bucket, the Savior told her that "whosoever drinketh of this water [the water she was pulling out of the well] shall thirst again: But whosoever drinketh of the water that I shall give him shall never thirst" (vv. 13–14). When we try to draw water out of the wells of the world, we will always be left wanting more. We will never be satisfied. Money doesn't do it, fame doesn't do it, and neither does beauty. When we seek for these types of things, it never quenches the real thirst we have in our souls. Have you heard the phrase, "The grass is always greener on the other side"? No matter what worldly accomplishments we get in our life, someone is always richer, always more popular, and always better-looking. We will always feel like we are lacking. But how come? Maybe it is because our souls were made by God and are infinite. That means that only infinity could satisfy them.

WE LONG FOR GOD. NOTHING ELSE COULD SATISFY US. THE PROMISE OF ETERNAL LIFE THAT HE PROVIDES FILLS US IN A WAY THAT NOTHING ELSE CAN.

It is eternal acceptance and worth and promises that the world cannot give. Notice that at the end of the conversation Jesus had with the woman, she leaves the well with her waterpot left behind. But she left the well with what she truly needed.

With the Lord as your shepherd, you "shall not want."

King David tells us more: "THOUGH I WALK THROUGH THE VALLEY OF THE SHADOW OF DEATH, I WILL FEAR NO EVIL." What a line! I am not sure what the valley of the shadow of death is, but I never want to go there. I can imagine, though, that David is referring to the dark and dreadful things that can and do happen in this world—

FEAR, DEATH, ENEMIES, SIN, ANXIETY, loneliness, and crime.

King David experienced many of those. He had been to an actual valley to face his greatest fears. But look what he said. YOU WILL GO TO THESE PLACES AND NOT FEAR, FOR HE WILL BE WITH YOU. And He will have a rod and staff with him. A rod was used by a shepherd as a weapon in ancient times. Not as a beating stick for the sheep, but for their enemies. Shepherds were skilled at protecting and defending their sheep. THERE IS NO ENEMY THAT CAN PREVAIL OVER YOU WITH JESUS AS YOUR SHEPHERD. You never have to fear. And His staff? This is often drawn or shown as a hook. Sometimes Jesus needs to loop the hook around us to pull us back from the danger we are walking into. This might sound harsh (especially around the neck!), but it is always motivated by His love. He knows exactly how to both protect us and lead us away from harm.

And then the last line:

"Surely goodness and mercy shall follow me all the days of my life."

The Hebrew for the word *follow* in that verse can also be translated as "to chase." Like a leopard does after its prey. His love will not only follow you but will chase after you all of your life. HIS LOVE DOESN'T JUST ACCEPT YOU WHEN YOU COME TO HIM; HE GOES OUT LOOKING FOR YOU. He will chase after your love and devotion all His days. He will constantly invite you and persuade you to come into His care.

HE WILL NEVER GIVE UP ON YOU OR LET YOU GO. THIS LEAVES US WONDERING: >>> WHY WOULD HE DO THAT? <<<

Many years ago I read a story from Elder John R. Lasater. He was visiting the country of Morocco, where many shepherds still live and care for their sheep the way that shepherds did during biblical times. He shared a memory from one of his trips about a sheep who had been hit by a car that belonged to the king's motorcade. They all pulled over and found out that the sheep was pretty broken and bruised up, but still alive. According to the law of the land, the king was required to pay the man one hundred times the value of the sheep for hitting it. The catch was, though, if the shepherd accepted the money, he had to butcher the sheep and divide up the meat. Elder Lasater's guide and interpreter then said, "BUT THE OLD SHEPHERD WILL NOT ACCEPT THE MONEY. THEY NEVER DO… BECAUSE OF THE LOVE HE HAS FOR EACH OF HIS SHEEP." When the shepherd refused the payment, he picked up his sheep and wrapped him in his robes and continued to rub its head and repeat a word over and over.

When Elder Lasater asked what the shepherd was saying, the interpreter said,

"Oh, he is calling it by name. All of his sheep have a name, for he is their shepherd, and the good shepherds know each one of their sheep by name."[2]

Why would the shepherd do that? Why not take the cash? One hundred times the value!? Think of how many other sheep he could buy with that. His business could start booming! Or maybe he wants to get out of the sheep business. Go buy an NBA team or something. WHY GIVE UP ALL THAT MONEY FOR A SHEEP THAT WILL BE SO HARD TO TAKE CARE OF? And for a sheep that was dumb enough to walk into the road without looking both ways in the first place? To keep the sheep seems like bad business. BUT THIS WASN'T JUST ANY SHEEP; IT WAS HIS SHEEP.

"WHAT MAN OF YOU, HAVING AN HUNDRED SHEEP, IF HE LOSE ONE OF THEM, DOTH NOT LEAVE THE NINETY AND NINE IN THE WILDERNESS, AND GO AFTER THAT WHICH IS LOST, UNTIL HE FIND IT? AND WHEN HE HATH FOUND IT, HE LAYETH IT ON HIS SHOULDERS, REJOICING" (LUKE 15:4–5).

All of that for just one sheep?

Remember the story of Jack getting lost at the beginning of this chapter? During every terrifying moment of looking for him, of all the thoughts I had and emotions I  felt and prayers I said, not once did I think, "You know what, I am just going to leave him lost. He never finishes the dinner he complains about, he loses his shoes professionally, he leaves his Legos all over the stairs for me to step on in the middle of the night, and he takes up a room in the house I could use for a gym. He drains my money, time, and emotional energy. He can't do anything on his own, and I would be richer without him." As I ran around like a wild thing looking for him, not one of those thoughts or anything close to them went through my head. Why? Because he is not just a kid. HE iS MY KiD.

What if the king had offered the shepherd two hundred times the value of the sheep? Three hundred? It still wouldn't have been enough, because of the love he has for each of his sheep. Each one. He would look up at the king and say, "I could never. This is my sheep." The scriptures tell us the story of this same type of shepherd. A shepherd who cares that deeply for each of His sheep. The injured ones, the lost ones, and the helpless ones too. Maybe especially. And how deeply?

Enough to give His life.

"I am the good shepherd:
the good shepherd giveth his life for the sheep"
(John 10:11).

When Jesus gave His life for us in Gethsemane and on the cross, He showed us He was our true shepherd. He walked into the valley of the shadow of death to find us, rescue us from our enemy, and bring us home to heal us. But this was even more than just a one-time act—His caring and compassion are new every day.

In the early morning and into the late night,

through the freezing cold and blistering heat,

UP ON THE HIGHEST MOUNTAINS AND DOWN INTO THE LOWEST VALLEYS,

through breakups and bad test scores,

THROUGH DISAPPOINTMENTS AND LOST CHAMPIONSHIP GAMES,

through heartaches and heartbreaks,

THROUGH SICK AND SIN AND RAIN AND SNOW AND ICE,

He takes care of His wandering sheep.

HE DOES THIS THROUGH HEALING GRACE,
TENDER ENCOURAGING WHISPERS FROM THE SPIRIT,
MESSENGERS SENT TO UPLIFT AND
WALK BY US THROUGH HARDSHIP,
AND EVERY OTHER MANIFESTATION OF HIS LOVE.

He can and does lead us to the greener, better pastures of life and protect us from the deadly things of this world. We might be hurt, but He can heal. We might be lost, but He can find. Like a good shepherd does, He also knows each of us individually. He knows everything that we need, each of our names, and each of the nitty-gritty details of our lives. And He does something about them. Each one of them. For each one of us. You. Your friends. Your enemies. Me. And you know what? HE LIKES US. Even though we wander and get stuck upside down and are needy and expensive. Whenever we are lost or injured, or even if we wander off in rebellion, He comes looking. No, not just looking; He chases after us! And when He finds us—dirty, hungry, diseased, and cold—he doesn't flinch or recoil in disgust, or butcher us and sell us off, but picks us up, wraps us in His shepherd robes in a tender embrace, and carries us home to tend to our every need. WHAT A SHEPHERD WE HAVE! A Shepherd who is in all of the tiniest details of our lives. We need Him every hour, and He is available and willing for all twenty-four of them.

It might seem like bad business to an outsider. Why invest yourself in such needy animals with no thought of payback or thanks? But He wouldn't have it any other way. Because He is my Shepherd. And I am His needy yet adorable little sheep. AND SO ARE YOU.

THE WATCHFUL SHEPHERD

Watches over, knows, protects, and cares for His sheep.
Leads them to the wonderful parts of life.
Will always go looking for His sheep who are lost.

3

THE LIGHT OF THE WORLD

Ever since I was little, I have slept with a light on. This is probably not the manliest thing to admit, but I am low-key a little bit scared of the dark. It just creeps me out. Anything could be there. I hate windows you can't see through at night, walking to my car after dark, swimming in murky, deep water, or having to leave the tent to go to the bathroom during the night while camping. I wait until morning no matter how bad it is. And those Halloween corn mazes? No, sir. No, ma'am. I absolutely will not. I hate my house at night. **EVEN NON-SCARY THINGS ARE SCARY IN THE DARK.** The shadow of a plant can give you a heart attack. Usually I am the last one to go to sleep in my house, and when it's time for me to go upstairs to bed, I strategically turn off and on certain lights as I walk to my room to make sure I'm never in the dark. And I still feel like every step I take, something is going to grab my ankles. The worst part is getting to my bed from the bedroom door. I turn off the lights so quick and run and jump into the bed like an Olympic hurdler. And yes, true story, I still lean over and check under my bed before climbing under the covers. Thank goodness no one can see how you act in the dark. Because if there were a video of me getting into bed or of the times when I have to check out some noise downstairs after midnight, I would lose all credibility. There is absolutely nothing tough about me when the sun goes down. I just hate the dark. Does anyone actually like it, by the way? It is dangerous and cold and creepy. Your worst fears only come in the dark!

When the Savior died on the cross in Jerusalem, the Saints on the other side of the world—the ones we read about in the Book of Mormon—experienced the signs of His death. These included earthquakes, tempests, destruction, and—worst of all—THREE DAYS OF INTENSE DARKNESS (you can read about this in 3 Nephi 8). There was crying out and wailing in great fear, regret, and sadness. I guarantee half of all that commotion would have been from me if I were alive back then! The darkness was so thick they couldn't even light a candle. That is crazy dark. Isn't it interesting that darkness was a sign of His death? And nothing could get rid of it. No candles, fires, stars—nothing. Sometime after the darkness was gone, as the people were gathered around the temple in Bountiful, they saw a light surrounding a man descending from heaven. It was Jesus. With everyone's eyes and ears focused on Him, He introduced Himself. He said, "Behold, I am Jesus Christ. . . . I am the light and the life of the world" (3 Nephi 11:10–11).

WHEN JESUS DIED, THE NEPHITES EXPERIENCED OVERWHELMING DARKNESS. WHEN HE CAME TO VISIT THEM, RESURRECTED AND ALIVE IN GLORY, HE INTRODUCED HIMSELF AS THE LIGHT.

Isn't that fitting? When He was gone, there was darkness. When He was back, there was light. WITHOUT JESUS LIFE WOULD BE COLD, SCARY, AND CONFUSING. WITH HIM IT CAN BE WARM, COMFORTING, AND CLEAR. HE IS JUST LIKE THE SUN—THE LIGHT OF THE WORLD.

The sun is so wild when you think about it. It is so fascinating to me to think about this giant, life-giving fireball out in space that just shows up every morning without fail—and on schedule! Every single day. Think of everything the sun means to us. Without it, we would literally be dead. It warms the earth, gives life to plants and animals, gives us light to see, and even gives us energy.

The sun is incredible—but it doesn't hold a candle to the Son.

In 2017, here in the United States, we experienced a rare astronomical event—a solar eclipse. In case you didn't pay attention in science, a solar eclipse happens when the moon passes in between the earth and the sun and blocks the sun's light during the day. The day before the eclipse, I looked online to see what time it would be happening and noticed that the city I was in would experience a ninety to ninety-five percent block of the sun. There were other places farther north where you could see the full block of the sun, but because of the angles of the sun, moon, earth, and all that fancy space stuff, the moon would be covering only about ninety percent of it where I was. I thought that was going to be plenty! No need to drive north! It happened on the first day of school at the university I work near, and everyone was so excited to watch it happen. Classes were canceled and loads of people were outside wearing their special sunglasses that allow you to look directly into the sun during the eclipse. I stood with a group of friends and we counted down the minutes to the eclipse as if it were New Year's. Music was playing and the atmosphere was electric. Finally, the moon started to cross the face of the sun and everyone started to cheer. We all waited anxiously as it moved further and further, covering more and more of the sun. And then it came—the moment of the eclipse— and it had to be the most disappointing thing in the world. Nothing was different. Well, the lighting was a little funky, and the shadows from the tree leaves all had the crescent shape of the moon in them, but overall it was pretty underwhelming. Our group of friends looked around at each other with an unimpressed "Is that it?" look on our faces. We took some pictures, posted them to Instagram, and then went back to our day.

 Later that night I saw some other friends' pictures and videos who were in the areas where the sun was blocked one hundred percent. It was amazing. It was as dark as night, and they could even see the stars at noonday. They said the temperature dropped instantly, and it was one of the craziest things they had ever experienced. It blew me away that only five to ten percent of the sun could make such a difference.

I have thought a lot about this experience since it happened. I was certain that covering the majority of the sun would have a major effect on the light and warmth of the area I was in. But I was wrong.

THE SUN IS SO POWERFUL THAT EVEN
FIVE PERCENT OF IT CAN STILL LIGHT AND
WARM THE WORLD. JUST LIKE JESUS.

His light is powerful. He pours out His hope and grace on anyone and everyone. "For God so loved the world, that he gave his only begotten Son," John said (John 3:16). The whole world!

Moroni teaches us that everyone born into the world is born with the light of Christ (see Moroni 7:16). Some people call this a conscience, but it is really the influence of Jesus showing everyone the way to live and be happy.

IN EVERY COUNTRY, IN EVERY CITY, AND EVERY HOUSE IN THE WORLD, JESUS IS PERSUADING AND GUIDING AND SHOWING THE WAY TO THE PEOPLE OF THE WORLD.

As they make decisions, they feel something inside pointing them the right way. They see more clearly what they should do. He is the light that is providing the clarity and direction.

Light also has the power to warm and comfort us. When Joseph Smith described seeing the Lord in the Kirtland Temple, one of the things he said was that He had eyes "as a flame of fire" (D&C 110:3). At first, that seems like a pretty freaky description, if you ask me! A person with fire eyes is precisely what I do not want to find under my bed in the night. But THINK ABOUT THE FEELING YOU GET AROUND A CAMPFIRE. Everyone is drawn to it. It warms you on a cold night. You can't help but stare into it. It is fascinating and mesmerizing and unexplainable. You feel protected when you are near it. I think Joseph may have been trying to describe those kinds of feelings that he got when he looked into His eyes.

Several years ago, I got a call from my friend telling me that her husband and a group of our friends had not come home when they were expected. The three of them were in the backcountry snowmobiling when they got turned around in the thousands of acres of trees and snow. Once they realized they were lost and the sun was going down behind the mountain, they knew they needed to build a fire if they were going to make it through the night. As my friend later looked back on his memory of that night, he made an interesting observation I will never forget.

He said that as long as the fire was blazing, they felt protected and warm and were laughing and telling stories in good spirits.

When the fire started to flicker and die, they would sit quietly, heads down, and get worried and depressed as the minutes passed. When they found a new dry log to add to the fire and the flames began to build again, so did their optimism. Their spirits rose and fell with the strength of the fire—they rose and fell with light.

LIGHT BRINGS HOPE.

It brings promise. It brings security. Just like Jesus does.

WHEN WE FEEL THE PRESENCE OF HIS SPIRIT, IT WARMS US AND COMFORTS US JUST LIKE A FIRE DOES.

Light, incredibly, also has the ability to chase away darkness. As you already know, this might be my favorite thing about it. All the darkness in the whole universe cannot swallow up the light of a single candle (unless Jesus is trying to teach a lesson, like He did with the Nephites).

LIGHT ALWAYS WINS.

We use the word *darkness* to talk about emotional and spiritual trials that we experience. We say things like, "That person was going through a dark time in his life." Darkness is hopelessness, fear, and danger.

In our lives, WE WILL ALL EXPERIENCE MOMENTS OF DARKNESS. There will be times when we want something so desperately, and then we will watch it slip through our fingertips. There will be other days when we won't know what to choose or where to go. We will be filled with doubt or worry or confusion. There will be people who disappoint us. There will be times when we feel lonely or unloved. Someone may leave you. Someone may hurt you. And sometimes it may feel like everyone and everything is going against you. There is a lot to be scared of or worried about in this world. These are all feelings and experiences we associate with darkness. We all have them, even Jesus's closest disciples.

Do you remember that super freaky night the disciples had out on the stormy sea? You can read more of the adventure in Matthew 14. Jesus  had told them He would meet them on the other shore, so they hopped in their boat and started rowing through the night. This was their first mistake—rowing in the dark! As they rowed, a storm started brewing and the waves started to pick up. Soon enough there were giant water walls crashing against their little wooden fishing boat, rocking them like a bucking bronco. They started to get a little spooked. Keep in mind, these were experienced fishermen. This wasn't their first water rodeo. If tourists on some Galilee Cruise start to worry about some waves, they are probably overreacting. But when fishermen who spend their lives on the water start to worry, you know you are in trouble. This wild weather went on for hours, and right at the peak of the fishermen's exhaustion from battling the waves, as if the frightening storm weren't enough, they look out across the water and see a figure walking toward them. In the middle of the night, remember! Matthew says they "CRIED OUT FOR FEAR" (Matthew 14:26). That means they made an audible, out-loud noise because of how scared they were. THEY SCREAMED. Grown men. Grown fishermen. One of those yells that starts in the gut and just comes out with the shakes. They were being rocked around for hours on the boat, and now, all of a sudden, a ghost shows up walking on the water. This story is my worst nightmare. But then, surprisingly, the figure speaks. A voice calls out from the waves:

"Be of good cheer; it is I; be not afraid" (v. 27).

Be not afraid?! Have cheer?? Are you kidding me? Everything that could ever be going wrong was going wrong at that moment.

THEY WERE COLD, WET, TIRED, AFRAID, AND LOST AT SEA. It was the middle of the night, in the middle of the water, in the middle of a storm. And if that wasn't scary enough, what they probably thought was some demon apparition was riding across the water coming to get 'em. Of course a ghost would tell them not to be afraid if it were on its way to eat them alive. There is nothing you could say to me in that moment to cheer me up. I would have dropped dead with fear or leapt myself right over the edge into the water. I am out. Done. Game over.

BE NOT AFRAID?

IMPOSSIBLE. UNLESS, OF COURSE,
THE ONE SAYING IT IS JESUS.

And that is exactly who it was. It was a familiar voice—a comforting voice—like a soothing lullaby. This is why the disciples start to settle.

JESUS HAD COME IN THE MIDDLE OF THE STORM, IN THE MIDDLE OF THE NIGHT, IN THE MIDDLE OF ALL THEIR FEARS. IT WAS NOT WHAT HE SAID THAT CALMED THEM DOWN; IT WAS WHO HE WAS.

To me, His most comforting line from the waves was "IT IS I." In other words, "Cheer up, boys! It's me. There is nothing to be afraid of anymore." Like someone seeing a light at the end of a tunnel, the disciples see Him and know that EVERYTHING IS GOING TO BE OKAY.

I recently heard one of Jesus's living disciples, Elder Ronald A. Rasband, say, "Try just saying the name 'Jesus Christ' in a perilous setting with one who has lost hope. Just calling upon Him by name, with reverence, can make a difference in a difficult moment."[3]

Just His name can bring comfort, relief, and reassurance. This is because, just like with a candle, all the evil and darkness and tragedy and hopelessness in the world are not powerful enough to snuff out the light and hope and answers that Jesus can bring.

Oh, and Jesus's enemies tried! They tried to stop Him when He was here on the earth. You can read about this in each of the four Gospel accounts. My favorite is in the Gospel of John, chapters 19 and 20. The disciples had followed Jesus and been with Him for three meaningful, unforgettable years. He filled their hearts with promises and left their memories dotted with miracles. And then He was gone. Just like that. He was captured and crucified. As they closed His tomb with a big rock, it must have felt like their hopes and dreams were buried inside with Him. He was gone, and none of them knew what to do next, where to go, or what to believe. IT WAS A DARK, WORRY-FILLED FRIDAY NIGHT. A night that could represent all of the darkness we may experience in our lives—the confusion, trouble, or loneliness that can be so common during our life on earth.

BUT THEN CAME SUNDAY MORNING.

I have always loved that Mary Magdalene, a disciple and close friend of Jesus, went to His tomb on the first Easter Sunday in the morning—right when the first sun rays begin to shoo away the darkness. When she arrived, she stumbled upon something that took her breath away: an empty tomb. The rock was rolled away, and the place where Jesus's body once was now had only the burial clothing lying there. No Jesus. When Mary first saw the empty tomb, she thought someone had stolen His body. She saw the empty tomb as a sign of grief, defeat, and despair. This was a new low. As she sat and cried in the garden, Jesus came and gently called her by name (see John 20:16).

In that moment, everything changed. That is a pattern with Him. He was not only there with her, but He was back from the grave.

Resurrected, alive, and standing before her. Can you imagine the feelings that were bouncing in her heart when she saw Him? SHE WAS NOT ALONE IN THE DARK ANYMORE, but was standing in that garden with the Light of the World. Imagine the security she felt seeing Him there. She may not have known how, but because of Jesus's Resurrection, everything was going to be okay. His empty tomb was actually a sign of hope. With the rock rolled away, light could fill the dark places.

The Light of the World was not locked away in a grave, but living, breathing, and ministering to her in that very moment.

Jesus said, "Be not afraid!" There is nothing on this earth or in this universe that can have power over you anymore. Even death—the greatest of all fears—had been so permanent and so final. NOW IT HAD BEEN CONQUERED. And if the greatest fear and enemy was now gone, all others could disappear with it. No matter what a person's problems are, NO MATTER HOW DARK OF A NIGHT IT IS, THAT DARKNESS IS ALWAYS SWALLOWED UP IN THE RISING OF THE MORNING SUN.

And so it is with Jesus.

BECAUSE OF HIM, THERE IS NO SIN, NO TRAGEDY, NO REBELLION, DESPAIR, OR SADNESS THAT HAS TO BE PERMANENT. THERE IS NOTHING TO BE AFRAID OF. IF HE CAN OVERCOME DEATH, HE CAN OVERCOME ANYTHING.

Hope came into the world with the Easter morning sun. Hope came walking out to those disciples on the stormy sea. It came into the world with Jesus. He is the light and the life and the hope of the world. Oh, there is so much to be afraid of. You might feel like you are those disciples out on the sea. It's dark. It's windy. Anything could happen! What if my parents get a divorce? What if I can't ever break this addiction? What if no one ever loves me? What if someone disappoints me or hurts me or leaves me? His light can shatter your fears and light up your way with answers, comfort, and reassurance that only He can bring. "BE OF GOOD CHEER," He says. Whatever happens, "I'm here!" Because of Him, each new day brings a promise of life and hope and warmth. "Weeping may endure for a night, but joy cometh in the morning" (Psalm 30:5). Because of Jesus, that joy is something we can anticipate and look forward to. His light is life, hope, faith, grace, and mercy. It is the influence of His presence and the power of His love. It can always be there.

Just like the sliver of light on the eclipse day, any amount of the Light of the World in our lives can bring a more powerful influence than we may anticipate. EVEN THE WHISPER OF JESUS'S NAME CAN BRING HOPE AND PEACE AND STRENGTH. However, the more of His influence or light we have and allow into our lives, the greater the security and mercy and grace and faith we can feel. "That which is of God is light; and he that receiveth light, and continueth in God, receiveth more light; and that light groweth brighter and brighter until the perfect day" (D&C 50:24). WE HAVE THE OPPORTUNITY TO PUT OURSELVES iN PLACES WHERE WE CAN FEEL AND EXPERiENCE MORE OF HiS LiGHT. His Spirit is light, so the more places we go and the more things we do that have His influence and Spirit in them, the more His light will be in our lives. And that light can grow brighter and brighter until the perfect day when we can be filled with it.

If you ever feel lost, look to Him. His light can guide you back. If you ever feel cold or afraid, come closer to Him. He will warm your heart. If you ever feel despair, listen to His words. He will be your hope.

There is nothing so scary or threatening in this world, in your life, or under my bed at night that it can stand against the light of Christ and come out victorious. His light is too great. He is the light of the whole world.

THE LIGHT OF THE WORLD

Fills us with hope and reassurance.
Chases away our darkness and fears.
Shows us the way.

4

THE EVER-PRESENT EMMANUEL

You probably already know this, but in case you don't, before a temple is dedicated, anybody is invited and allowed to go visit and walk through the rooms inside during an open house. I am not allowed to walk through any of my friends' houses at will, so it is pretty rad that the Lord invites everyone to just walk through all of His. They put these little white booties on your feet and you just stroll through the big hallways and grand staircases. You feel so fancy. If you ever get a chance, take it! And bring all your friends. **TEMPLES ARE SET APART AND SET ASIDE TO BE HOLY PLACES OF BEAUTY, LIGHT, AND GRACE.** And the chandeliers in them are out of this world—some of them bigger than my whole living room. And they usually have free cookies at the end. Double bonus. Lucky for us, we have been living near several temples for these open houses and have been able to go and walk through them with our kids. This is usually an adventure, shuffling six wild things through a really clean and expensive house. But we have loved it—even the time Christian thought the baptismal font was a swimming pool and snuck under the ropes and ran full speed to go jumping in. Luckily, at the last second a nice lady grabbed his arm and prevented a catastrophe. Bless her. He didn't know how to swim, so that would have led to at least two of us being the first ones fully immersed in that font.

Another open house moment that I will not forget is when my daughter asked on the way to the temple if we would **SEE JESUS WHEN**

WE WENT iNSiDE. The thought thrilled her. It was His house, after all—why wouldn't He be home? All I said was, "Why not? You never know." She rode in bubbling anticipation. I remember thinking that same thing when I was younger too. I was positive that Jesus lived in the temple. Every closed door I passed by my first time through made me wonder if it was His bedroom. I even knocked on one to see if He would open. He never did. And I never saw Him.

BUT I FELT
LIKE HE WAS THERE.

I feel like that every time I go.

When Matthew started his book about the life of Jesus, he told the story of His birth and quoted the Old Testament prophet Isaiah, who gave the Lord a name six hundred years before He ever came. He said, "Behold, a virgin shall be with child, and shall bring forth a son, and they

> shall call his name Emmanuel,
> which being interpreted is, God with us"
> (Matthew 1:23).

The Hebrew word and name that Isaiah gave Him—*Emmanuel*—literally means, "God is with us."

WHEN JESUS WAS BORN IN BETHLEHEM,
THE GOD OF HEAVEN LITERALLY CAME TO
THE WORLD TO BE WITH US.

Do you remember our chapter on Jehovah? On the first Christmas morning, that same Lord and God of the Old Testament came down to the world as a baby. THE VERY SAME PERSON. He left His throne and mansion and glory on high and came into a mortal body. It fascinates me to think that when Mary held Him for the first time, she was holding the Creator of the world. When Isaiah saw the first Christmas in vision, he saw a picture of God coming to the world to be with His people. In the flesh.

PEOPLE ACTUALLY TALKED WITH HIM FACE-TO-FACE, LIVED NEXT DOOR TO HIM, AND WALKED NEXT TO HIM DOWN DUSTY ROADS. HE WAS HERE. GOD WITH US. DURING HIS EARTHLY MINISTRY, HE LITERALLY AND PHYSICALLY WAS WITH HIS PEOPLE.

Even though He walked on the earth for only about thirty years as a human, HE IS STILL EMMANUEL. This is who He has always been and will always be.

> HE IS NOT A DISTANT GOD OUT IN THE CORNER OF THE UNIVERSE, BUT HERE WITH US AND NEAR US IN OUR LIVES.

Do you remember the story of Shadrach, Meshach, and Abednego? Those are some names! These were Hebrew boys who had been kidnapped and taken into Babylon, a neighbor enemy to Israel. Can you even imagine someone coming and snatching you from your hometown and taking you off to a foreign country where you don't speak the language, know the food, or know what is even going to happen to you? They were taken away so they could be re-raised as Babylonians. They were taught, fed, and cultured to be like the people in their new country. It didn't take long, though, for the authorities in Babylon to recognize what studs these boys were, and soon they were promoted and made princes and governors over some of the states of the country. Around that time, the king of Babylon, Nebuchadnezzar, had a giant, ninety-foot golden statue made and invited all the leaders to come for the unveiling and dedication of it. This must have been the hot ticket in Babylon that year. Everybody who was anybody was coming. The elite. There must have been shrimp cocktails, and a red carpet, glitzy outfits, and fancy reporters. They even had a concert planned—the Babylon Grammys. When they got there, in the shadow of this glittering statue, the emcee of the event announced to everyone that when the music started to play, everyone was commanded to bow down and worship the idol.

Shadrach, Meshach, and Abed-nego had grown up with their hearts set on God alone.

Even if everyone else bowed down to the golden man, they planned on reserving their bended knees for Jehovah alone. And that's what happened. You can read this whole story in Daniel chapter 3. And you will read that when the music started playing, and all the princes and governors and leaders bowed down in worship, THREE LONE BOYS STAYED STANDING. That doesn't seem like that big of a deal, unless you read that there was a consequence for anyone who didn't bow. They weren't just kicked out of the party. Not just shunned or cast out from the crowd. BUT THROWN INTO AN OVEN. They would be fired. Literally. So when those three stood there, tall as trees, some of the others noticed. How could you not? And they went and tattled on them to the king. "Those Jewish kids aren't bowing down! They are defying you!"

Oh, the king threw a fit! He came storming over, demanding the boys kneel down. But they wouldn't. He raged on them—"Don't you know I could burn you up for disobeying?" Yep, they knew. They said to the king,

"If it be so,"—if you decide to burn us up—"our God whom we serve is able to deliver us . . . and he will. . . . But if not, be it known unto thee, . . . we will not serve thy gods, nor worship the golden image" (Daniel 3:17–18).

These boys!! I love them. Our God can save us from your oven, they said, but even if He chooses not to, we still won't bow down.

The king ordered the fire to be heated up SEVEN TIMES HOTTER than usual. His temper matched the flames. It was so hot, the soldiers who opened the door got fried for just being close. CRISPY! The king had the boys tied up and thrown into the furnace. And then you'll love this part. Once the king brushed off his hands and sat down on his thrown to look into the fire with victory, he jumped right back up out of his seat as though he had sat on a tack. Servant! Servant, come here!

 "Did not we cast three men bound into the midst of the fire?"

Yes, sir, we did, sir, was the answer. And then the king said,

"Lo, I see four men loose, walking in the midst of the fire, and they have no hurt." I see four! One, two, three, four. "And the form of the fourth"—you will love this!—"is like the Son of God" (vv. 24–25).

The figure was like the Son of God, because it was the Son of God. Jesus, Emmanuel, GOD WHO WAS WITH THEM. Not watching from a distant throne, but there in the burning fiery furnace with them. Right there.

He is always showing up in the most unexpected places. Ovens, lion pits, tumbling prisons, and wilderness places. When He was born and came to the earth, He could've chosen anywhere to live, but

THE KING OF KINGS DECIDED TO BE BORN IN A STABLE,

and then lived most of His life on one of the poor streets on the other side of the tracks in small-town Nazareth. We might think that God only belongs or comes exclusively to temples, or churches, or other fancy, holy places. But that isn't true. He came first to a poor family in a cave for animals. If the angels had not told the shepherds where to find Jesus that first Christmas night, THEY NEVER WOULD HAVE GONE LOOKING FOR HIM IN A BETHLEHEM BARN. They would've gone to a synagogue or the temple mount. "In this place?" they would've asked. "In these conditions??" Yes, shepherds. Even in this place. Especially in these types of conditions. Why?

BECAUSE HE CAME TO BE WITH US. WHERE WE ARE.
IN OUR BARNS AND IN OUR MESSES.
WHERE HE CHOOSES TO BE IS AN INDICATION
OF WHAT HE CARES ABOUT. OF WHO HE CARES ABOUT.

Matthew, who quoted the name Emmanuel, also wrote about a promise that Jesus gave to His disciples at the end of His life before

He left the earth. "I AM WITH YOU ALWAY, EVEN UNTO THE END OF THE WORLD" (Matthew 28:20). Seems like a powerful promise, right? I was here with you, and I will still be with you always. The funny thing about this promise is that right after He said it, He left them. Flew up to heaven. Gone. It makes me laugh when I play out the scene.

Jesus gave them all one last big hug and then a promise: "I will never leave you." And then He leaves. ⟹

Well . . . what did the disciples think standing there on the Mount of Olives? I just picture them looking up. WAITING. Kind of side glancing at each other. Someone mumbles out a *hmmm*. Who spoke up first? Peter? Certainly He wasn't breaking a promise two seconds after He made it. JESUS PROMISED that He, God, would be with them always. AND HE DOESN'T LIE. He said that He would not just casually observe their stories, but that He would be present in their stories. Right by them.

SO WHAT ABOUT WHEN HE IS GONE OR WHEN YOU CAN'T SEE HIM THERE?

Sometimes it feels like He isn't really there. We often feel alone in our journeys and wonder why He isn't there. Well, let me help you see this. Do you remember the story of ESTHER? It would most certainly be voted one of the TOP TEN BEST STORIES FROM THE BIBLE. If you haven't read it in a while, you might want to go snuggle up with a blanket on the couch and go through it again. It is really easy to find—just look for Esther in the Old Testament. It isn't very long, and it is a page turner! When you are done reading it, you feel like you just watched a blockbuster movie—

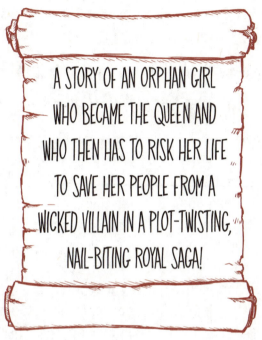

A STORY OF AN ORPHAN GIRL WHO BECAME THE QUEEN AND WHO THEN HAS TO RISK HER LIFE TO SAVE HER PEOPLE FROM A WICKED VILLAIN IN A PLOT-TWISTING, NAIL-BITING ROYAL SAGA!

It is good stuff! Esther was a Jew who grew up in the Persian empire. When the Persian king divorced his wife Vashti, he went on a search through the kingdom for another bride. He found Esther, a poor girl from the slums, and she became the Queen of Persia. One of the king's advisors, Haman, hated the Jews and plotted a scheme to have all of them killed. As the day of execution approached, Esther's uncle Mordecai encouraged her to go before the king and plead for their lives. She responded with a harsh reality. SHE COULDN'T DO IT. Not only did the king not know Esther was a Jew, but on top of that, Persia was in a state of war and because of the fear of spies and treason, IT WAS AGAINST THE LAW FOR ANYONE TO ENTER THE THRONE ROOM OF THE KING UNINVITED. That was a crime punishable by death. It had been thirty days since Esther had even seen the king. Mordecai's request was not a simple or safe one. When he wrote her again, he told her she was their only hope, and he ended it by saying,

"Who knoweth whether thou art come to the kingdom for such a time as this?" (Esther 4:14).

Esther, maybe you are there for a reason, he was saying. This reason. Esther was gifted great courage, gathered her maidens to fast, and against all odds and reason went to the king uninvited with the battle cry, "If I perish, I perish" (v. 16). Can you imagine what that moment was like when the doors to the king's chambers creaked open? Not all stories in the scriptures end with a happily ever after, but  this one did. The king granted her permission to enter and then heard the plea of his wife on behalf of her people. THEY WERE SAVED! Jewish people all over the world still celebrate that day and that miracle with parades and parties on a holiday called Purim.

That is one of my favorite stories, but here is the crazy part (and the reason I told it to you!). DID YOU KNOW THAT THE BOOK OF ESTHER NEVER MENTIONS THE NAME OF GOD? Not once. Go check it out. Not by any of His names. Isn't that wild? There are some who wonder why it is even in the Bible at all. Why have a story that doesn't mention God in a book that was put together for the sole purpose of teaching us about God?? How did it make the cut?

Let me ask you something. Even though it doesn't mention Him, and even though they never see Him, DOES IT MEAN GOD WASN'T THERE? Did He bail on Esther and her people? Did He abandon them in their hardest hour? Was He asleep? On vacation? Was He off in some other corner of the universe? What do you think? WAS GOD INVOLVED IN HER STORY?

Of course He was! Just look at the facts!

Do you think it was a coincidence that out of all the available girls in the kingdom, Esther was chosen as queen? What are the odds that a Jewish girl is picked to live in the palace at the same time a plot is hatched to destroy all the Jews? Wasn't it the Lord who set that all up?

Don't you think He was there arranging it all behind the scenes—putting each piece of the puzzle in its place until it was set up perfectly?

And wasn't He there by her side when she risked her life to go before the king uninvited—softening the king's heart and filling hers with courage? Can't you just see Him walking next to her as she walked down that long hallway to the throne room, whispering in her ear, "You've got this, my dear!" Of course He was there! Those are His people in the story! We are all His people! At first glance, what might seem like a story of a distant or quiet or nonexistent God is actually a story of the great rescue of an entire nation by an ever-present and very concerned Emmanuel.

In fact, there is not a page of the Bible or a page in history when God has not been involved. He is always there.

I have wondered if the writers of that book left His name out on purpose to teach us that just because you don't see Him at first glance doesn't mean He isn't there.

So how do we see Him more? How do we notice Him? A few years ago my friend Devin and I were texting back and forth when he ended the conversation with a "good night" and a sunflower emoji. I laughed because it was so random and asked what the sunflower meant. He texted back: "I don't know. It just makes me happy when I see them. Aren't they so happy?"

I laughed out loud. "Yep, they are," I texted back.

"I think I am going to start sending that emoji to people," he said. "It's gonna be my thing."

I laughed out loud again, sent a sunflower emoji back, and went to bed.

The next day I was driving to work and passed by a field of sunflowers and immediately thought about Devin. (And they really did make me happy!) I pulled over and took a quick picture and sent it to him. He loved it. And then it began. It became a thing. Funny enough, I don't think I had ever really noticed sunflowers before that conversation. They grow like crazy in the field behind my house, but I had never really seen them. Now I see them everywhere. And every time I do I think about Devin and it makes me happy.

ONCE I STARTED LOOKING FOR SUNFLOWERS, I NOTICED THEM.

They had been there all along, but until Devin helped me start seeing them, they had never stood out to me or had any impact on me at all. I have had similar thoughts about Jesus. I BELIEVE HIS PROMISE TO US, HIS DISCIPLES, THAT HE WOULD BE THERE ALWAYS. I also believe Isaiah's name for Him is still accurate.

God with us. He is in everything, He is present, and He is Emmanuel.

Sometimes I need to be looking for Him and watching for His hand and His influence in my story if I want to see Him there. Nephi wrote at the beginning of the Book of Mormon that it was his purpose to

"SHOW UNTO YOU THAT THE TENDER MERCIES OF THE LORD ARE OVER ALL THOSE WHOM HE HATH CHOSEN"
(1 NEPHI 1:20).

That was going to be a theme of his writing. A constant witness of the hand of the Lord in their lives. At the end of the book, Moroni asks the readers to "remember how merciful the Lord hath been unto the children of men, from the creation of Adam even down until the time that ye shall receive these things" (Moroni 10:3). I love those bookend challenges. At the beginning, Nephi asks us to LOOK FOR THE TENDER MERCIES in the book, and Moroni asks us to REMEMBER THEM when we finish. Watch for the hand of the Lord, they both say. And both of them say it with a spirit of promise that you and I will be witnesses of Him as we do so. That we will notice Him. One of my favorite readings of the Book of Mormon was a time when I went through with a yellow pencil and marked every time I saw the Lord present in the stories of that book. I marked times He answered prayers, times He sent angels, times He performed miracles, times He gave inspiration, dreams, voices, and feelings of comfort, forgiveness, and grace. I marked as many of the tender mercies that I could find—the big ones and the little ones. I WAS OVERWHELMED BY HOW OFTEN I SAW HIM IN THAT BOOK. Every page was colored yellow! I had no idea. You might want to try it sometime.

One of the best things that came from that experience was a greater ability to SEE HiM iN MY OWN STORY. I got into the habit every night, after checking under my bed for creepy things and then hopping into the covers, to try to

think about when I had seen His influence in my life that day

—times when He had been with me.[4] The more I do it, the more I have been able to spot His subtle yet significant presence more easily. Like the day I remembered feeling courage surge into me right before I went into an intimidating situation. Or that other day when a song came on the radio with the very message that I needed. Or the day I felt forgiveness for something I had said in anger. I STARTED NOTiCiNG THAT GOD WAS STiLL WiTH US. Still with me. Whenever I notice Him in one of these moments I will usually mumble under my breath,

⟹ "I SEE YOU,"

just as a way to let Him know that I know He is there. Noticing and remembering has helped me to see Him even more. I am finding that He has been there all along—like sunflowers growing in my backyard. I live with more confidence and I live with more concern for His purposes because of it.

A year ago, one of my best friends, Isaac, found the Lord present in His story. At the end of his senior year, everything was on the up-and-up. Graduation was right around the corner, all of the end-of-the-year dances and activities were in full swing, and he had a mission call to serve for twenty-four months in the England London South Mission. He was on top of the world. It was such a brilliant time. One night, at his younger brother's choir concert, his mom turned to him and he could immediately tell something was wrong. He helped her out to the hallway, and right there against the lockers he gave his first priesthood blessing. After some testing at the hospital, the diagnosis came back. She had a brain tumor, and the doctors estimated she had eighteen to twenty-four months to live. We all cried, prayers were offered, and hearts were broken. As treatments began and all the initial shock began to pass, Isaac knew he needed to make a decision about his mission call. He wanted to be a missionary so badly, but he also knew he might need to stay home. What was the answer? They both seemed right.

One afternoon, Isaac decided he wanted to **GO TO THE TEMPLE** to just pray and think. On his way, he prayed that God would be present. He had no demands for the Lord. The Lord could help Isaac with his answer however and whenever He wanted, but **ISAAC JUST NEEDED TO KNOW THAT THE LORD WAS AWARE OF HIM AND THAT HE WAS WITH HIM.** He sat for a while in the waiting area of the temple before he decided that as long as he was there he might as well do some baptisms for the dead. He changed into his white jumper and went into the baptistry. As he stood in the font waiting to be baptized, he looked up at the name and information of the person he was going to be baptized for. That is when he noticed it. **SOMMERSET COUNTY.** The person he was being baptized for was from a place smack-dab in the middle of the England London South Mission. And so was the second person. And the third. And the fourth. And the fifth. All of them were from little towns right in the middle of the mission he had been called to.

He told me, "David, I felt like Joseph Smith in the Sacred Grove—when God called him by name." **HE KNEW THAT GOD WAS AWARE. THAT GOD WAS PRESENT.** That He was with him. Just like He promised to His disciples so many years ago. Amazingly, when Isaac went to England, he was assigned to labor and serve in Sommerset County.

I SEE YOU.

Not long after Isaac returned home, his mom passed away peacefully in her sleep. The Lord could've healed her—I am certain of that—but just because He didn't, doesn't mean He doesn't care and it doesn't mean He wasn't there. Because He was. That is the Jesus we know and love. A Jesus that knows and loves us. And He shows us that love by being with us in our stories—no matter what they may look like.

You might feel His presence in the form of courage when you face a friend in trouble

or have to step out of your comfort zone.

YOU MIGHT FEEL HIM IN MOMENTS OF FORGIVENESS OR IN ENCOURAGING WHISPERS.

YOU MIGHT BE PROMPTED TO GO TO THE RESCUE OF SOMEONE IN NEED.

Or it might have been a hard day, and you will feel peace as you sit there at night—as if He is right there sitting on the edge of your bed.

And even if we don't see Him there at first glance, He is keeping His promise He made on the Mount of Olives before leaving—that He would be with us always.

On that day for Isaac, JESUS WAS iN THE TEMPLE, just like my daughter thought He was. He was there as Emmanuel. And He has been there and will be there for every other day, too.

In temples, in barns, in ovens, in messes—in our stories.

THE EVER-PRESENT EMMANUEL

Has been and will be with us in our stories.

Notices us and is always aware of us.

Will be near us whether we see Him or not.

5

THE TENDER JESUS

One morning, my wife, Jenny, asked our little girl Elle what she wanted to be when she grew up. Almost immediately she said, "A mom. Or a mermaid." Then she stopped what she was doing, looked up for a second, squished her face in deep thought, and then said a more determined, "But probably a mom. Because sharks." I died. But I appreciate the valid concern.

I am more than a third of the way through my life (I am shooting for 100) and am still not quite sure what I want to be when I grow up. There are so many options. For a while I thought about being a dentist like my dad—but I'm not sure if teeth do it for me. I love a good smile on someone, but I don't want to pick stuff off of them and drill into them. And I don't floss—so that would make me a hypocrite. Dentist is out. Let's see, what else has been on the table—astronaut, professional golfer, member of a boy band (that is still on the table), movie star, opening a smoothie shop, working at Harley Davidson, therapist, life coach, taking over for Jimmy Fallon someday, and most recently, a vanilla bean farmer. I probably should pick movie star so every movie I'm in I can be something different. People can't see inside my scattered brain, so sometimes they assume I am more responsible than I actually am and ask me for advice in choosing a career. Believe it or not, I do have some good advice: Job shadow. Follow someone for a few days. You can find out real fast whether you want to be a dentist or not by watching a dentist stare into mouths all day.

> ## NO MATTER WHAT I FINALLY CHOOSE TO BE WHEN I GROW UP, THE ONE PERSON I HOPE TO BE MORE LIKE IS JESUS.

One of the fan favorites in the Primary songbook is "I'm Trying to Be Like Jesus." What a song, right?! Well, what if? What if I really tried to be like Jesus? I wear one of those cool thread bracelets with the initials WWJD on it. It stands for "What would Jesus do?" Well, what's the answer to that? What would He do?

What if you could follow Him for a day or two—job shadow?

What if you could watch what He said, how He responded, and how He chose to spend His hours? What would you learn about Him? What is Jesus like? And what is it like to be like Him?

The name of *Jesus* is a Greek name. In Hebrew, it is translated from *Joshua*, which means

"GOD IS HELP" OR "THE LORD SAVES."[5]

I love these! Mary and Joseph didn't name Him on their own, by the way. (Lucky ducks! That is the hardest part of having kids, FYI—naming them. It is so permanent!) But these two were given Jesus's name by the angel Gabriel. IT WAS A NAME THAT TAUGHT WHO HE WOULD BE—one who would help and who would save. Like I said in an earlier chapter, during that time, there were lots of boys and men who were named Joshua or Jesus. It was a popular and common name and would not have caused people to turn their heads if they heard it spoken on the streets. That is different now.

Because of the way He lived His life, the name of Jesus has become a beautiful one.

It brings heart-stirring feelings because of the way He so deliberately dealt with people as He walked through the lands of Israel. The way He helped them and saved them so tenderly. THAT iS THE MEANING OF THE NAME OF JESUS TODAY: TENDER LOVE.

I think Matthew, Mark, Luke, and John should all get an extra indoor swimming pool or fancy pebble ice machine in their mansions in heaven for what they gave to the rest of us. THEY WROTE DOWN JESUS'S STORY FOR US. His biography. His day-to-day life on earth. And when you read it, it is filled with stories of compassionate detours, unexpected responses, and visits to places no one else would go. Helping and saving in the most gentle and tender of ways.

One single story of Jesus could teach us what that name means and has the power to melt our hearts and win us over to Him.

He always knew the way to people's hearts. As I read through the New Testament, it always surprises me how good He actually is, and it causes me to wish more and more to have Him in my own story. Here are some of my FAVORITE MOMENTS from some of my recent job shadowing of Jesus in the Gospels. Here are some of the reasons why that name means so much to me today.

The FIRST STORY is told best in the Gospel of Mark. Right in the beginning. Mark 1. Somewhere on the dusty streets, there was a MAN WHO WAS PLAGUED WITH LEPROSY. Leprosy was a horrible disease. It caused your body to first ache in pain and eventually rot and fall apart. Like literally body parts falling off the body. In those days, there was no cure for it.

Most lepers carried a bell around because it was the law to warn anyone coming close to them that they were a leper. They would yell out, "Unclean, unclean!" as others approached (see Leviticus 13:45–48). People in ancient times avoided lepers like they would a leopard—the dangerous jungle cat with sharp teeth. If you accidentally came in contact with a leper, you had to go through a long waiting period and drawn-out cleansing process to be able to enter society again. The disease was super contagious and could easily be passed from person to person. All it took was one wrong brush against a leper and your life could be ruined or over. If you saw a leper, you grabbed your friend's arm and you ran.

Because they were unclean, lepers were forced to wear certain clothes that marked them as dangerous and diseased, and they were cast out to live outside the main parts of the city—away from everyone else. I imagine it could have been years since the man in the story had had any close contact with another human being.

No friendly handshakes. No warm hugs. No kisses good night.

HE WAS UNTOUCHABLE.

His body ached fiercely, but his heart ached even more.

The rags that hung off his body were a reflection of his life—falling apart.

But when the man with leprosy saw that Jesus was near, he ran.

HE RAN TO JESUS. He hurried in His direction, fell at His feet, and begged Him for a chance at a different life.

"If thou wilt, thou canst make me clean" (Mark 1:40).

Every time I read that story, I wonder what the leper had heard about Jesus that made him want to run to Him.

That made him think he was even allowed to. This man was at the bottom of the totem pole. He was considered by many to be a nobody with nowhere to go. He was a walking plague. And in this story, a running one. Others may have sneered—most may have sneered—

BUT JESUS HAD SYMPATHY.

"And Jesus, moved with compassion, put forth his hand, and touched him, and saith unto him, I will; be thou clean" (v. 41).

If you will, the leper asked, as if most people wouldn't. I will, Jesus answered, letting Him know He wasn't like most people.

Did you notice how Jesus healed him? He is all-powerful and uniquely creative. There are lists of different ways He could have shown His miraculous power to heal the man's leprosy. He could have simply spoken the words and the man would've been healed. He could have waved His hand over him like a magic wand and the disease would have been gone. Instead,

He touched him. That is how He chose to restore the man's life— with a tender touch to an untouchable man.

My friend's mom once told me a story about her little girl that I always want to remember. This mom used to visit a lady in the neighborhood on occasion. She was an older woman who had been in a fire earlier in her life that had left her face, neck, and arms all scarred and flaky. SHE GOT DOUBLE TAKES AND STARES when she left the house to go the grocery store. My friend had a standing lunch date with her once a month, and on one of those afternoons, her daughter's babysitter fell through and she could not find anyone who could watch her. She hated to cancel the appointment, but she was afraid of what her daughter's reaction would be if she saw the woman. What if she snarled her face? What if she was scared and ran? WHAT IF SHE SAID SOMETHING TACTLESS LIKE KIDS DO? The mom decided to go over to the house anyway and tried to explain over and over to her daughter what the older woman looked like to prepare her for the shock. They walked up to the front door and rang the bell. As they waited for the woman to come, the mom gave her daughter one more lesson on manners. Someone else opened the door, and the two of them walked into the living room where the woman was sitting in her chair. My friend's little girl walked straight to the chair and climbed up onto the woman's lap. She put both her little hands on the scarred cheeks of the old woman, looked at her face, gently rubbed one side, and said, holding her other hand to her cheek (while her mom held her breath), "YOU ARE SO PRETTY." Sometimes I think I know why Jesus liked to hang out with little kids. They see people the way He does.

You might be treated like an outcast—avoided because you are physically or spiritually falling apart.

YOU MAY FEEL UNTOUCHABLE OR UNAPPROACHABLE TO OTHERS, BUT NOT TO JESUS.

He sees pretty where others see the plague. When the world treats some as trash, Jesus picks them up with tenderness.

On another day and in ANOTHER STORY, Jesus went to a surprising place on the other side of the sea. Mark tells this story really well too. You can find it in Mark 5. The place He went was a place called the Gadarenes. The Gadarenes were the bad part of town. The place you never want to get a flat tire. The place you never want to go—especially at night! There on the other side of the tracks was A MAN POSSESSED WITH EVIL SPIRITS who lived in the graveyard. Chains hung off of his body like a Halloween costume, rattling the rocks as he moved through the tombs. The people of the village had tried to tame him and chain him down—like a wild animal—but he had broken free. "And always, night and day, he was in the mountains, and in the tombs, crying, and cutting himself with stones" (Mark 5:5).

Freaky, right? I cannot even imagine what this man looked like. Cuts and scars, with chains and rags dangling off of his body. His hair and teeth were probably not brushed, and he must have smelled something fierce after sleeping in the cemetery all those nights. I wonder if the people from the nearby towns could hear his cries at night echoing through the mountain tombs. I know this was just a man, but his description always leaves me shaking in my boots.

I am fairly confident I would have avoided this place and this man at all costs.

BUT NOT JESUS.

The way Mark tells the story, it seems as if Jesus came to this place for one reason only—to see this man. Only He knows why He came, but He came. And when Jesus stepped out of His ship, the man came running to Him. Can you imagine getting out of your car and all of a sudden looking up to see a man like that running at you? I think I would've gone into a Karate Kid stance. But Jesus stood as calm as a morning and asked him something that has always touched my heart. I am not sure what His intentions were or if we have the whole conversation, but the first question that Mark records Jesus asking is, "WHAT iS THY NAME?" (Mark 5:9). What is your name? That is not the first question that comes to mind for me. "What are you?" or "Why are you runnin' at me?" are the first questions that I think of. But not Jesus. He sees past that.

HE SAW THE WONDERFUL UNDER THE WILD.

After a short conversation, Jesus cast the devils out of the man and healed him. It was not long before the people of the village were shocked at the sight of the wild man "sitting, and clothed, and in his right mind" (v. 15). Just like that. A totally different person. That seems common with people who meet Jesus.

I once had a friend ask me,

"If Jesus were in our city today, and we had to try to find Him, where do you think you would go?"

Would you be more likely to see Him in church or under the freeway with an arm around a man holding a cardboard sign—asking him his name? Some may feel abandoned or plagued with devils of sin, sickness, or addiction.

Everyone else might think you are a lost cause—but not Jesus.

He has a way to help and a way to save. And He comes in close to do it.

Jesus seemed to always be shocking everyone with who He talked to, spent time with, and invited into His circles. In chapter 19 of Luke's job shadow of Jesus, we meet A MAN NAMED ZACCHAEUS. He was A TAX COLLECTOR. A thug in the ancient world. No one liked the tax collectors. They were usually dirty, rotten scoundrels. Cheaters! They worked for Rome and they were considered traitors. Plus, they took your money! Zacchaeus was not just any tax collector—he was a chief tax collector, which means he was at the top of the food chain. Rich. Famous. The big guy in Jericho. Everyone may have hated him, but he could deal with it lounging by his pool in his fancy backyard.

One day, Jesus passed through Jericho, Zacchaeus's hometown. When Zacchaeus caught word of it, he ran to where Jesus was. He really wanted to meet Him, but he couldn't because of all the people that were around Him (see Luke 19:3). HIS PROBLEM? HE WAS TOO SHORT. He couldn't see over the crowd—a crowd he was not a part of. A crowd that probably wouldn't let him in anyway. And so he ran ahead to climb up into a tree so he could get a look as Jesus passed. Don't you love picturing that? A grown businessman climbing a sycamore tree! I love that he thinks outside the box and has childlike faith to see Him. "And when Jesus came to the place, he looked up, and saw him, and said unto him, Zacchaeus, make haste, and come down; for to day I must abide at thy house" (v. 5). What?

Zacchaeus was watching from the nosebleeds and got an invitation to the box seats—to have lunch with Jesus.

When I was in junior high, President Gordon B. Hinckley (the prophet at the time) came to Houston for a big Church meeting. There were so many people that we had to meet in the Astrodome, a sports arena where the MLB and NFL teams played. Thousands of people were there. When it was all done, President Hinckley got off the stage and hopped into a golf cart to take him across the field to the underground parking where his car was. As he rode, he looked right up in my direction. I was certain our eyes had met. **AND THEN HE WAVED! RIGHT AT ME! ME!** I started to wave back in amazement. I couldn't believe it was happening. The prophet was waving at me! I turned to my mom, who was standing next to me, to make sure she was seeing it! When I looked at her, she was waving too. It surprised me at first, and I wondered if she thought President Hinckley was waving at her instead of me. Silly mom. But then I looked next to her and saw that person waving, and the next person, and the next. I then turned the other direction and saw the whole row of people to my left waving too. It wasn't until I turned around and saw hundreds and hundreds of people waving behind me that I realized President Hinckley wasn't actually waving just to me. I was so bummed. It was so thrilling for just a second when President Hinckley was calling me out of the crowd. It made me feel chosen and important.

I didn't have a one-on-one with President Hinckley that day, but Zacchaeus did have a one-on-one with Jesus.

THE LORD DIDN'T JUST PASS BY AND WAVE UP INTO THE TREE; HE CALLED OUT TO HIM.

"Zacchaeus." His name. And then Jesus invited him to hurry down for lunch at his house. A one-on-one. I would love to know what they talked about! This lunch quickly became a scandal on the streets of Jericho. No one could believe that Jesus would want to go to Zacchaeus's house! Of all the people who lived there—him?! The thug? The little short guy? The cheat? The outsider? That guy doesn't even go to our church!

But there Jesus was sitting down with Zacchaeus for lunch. You might notice as you job shadow Jesus how often it mentions Him eating. In Jesus's day, eating with someone was known as a "table of fellowship." It was a way of showing that you accepted the people you were eating with. If they were at your table, they were your friends—just as they are, no matter who they were or what they did. Like school lunch, right? The people you eat lunch with are usually the group that you like, are like, or want to be like.

I wonder what table Jesus would sit down at in your school cafeteria.

Nephi seemed to think it would be anyone's table.

"And he inviteth them all to come unto him and partake of his goodness; and he denieth none that come unto him, black and white, bond and free, male and female; and he remembereth the heathen; and all are alike unto God" (2 Nephi 26:33).

He doesn't care what your race is, your social status, the number of followers you have, the amount of money you've got, or what church you go to. He doesn't care if you stink of sin or scandal or sickness. HE INVITES EVERYONE TO SIT AT HIS TABLE. And He invites them in the same tender way He did with Zacchaeus—not as big groups, but ONE BY ONE. Each and every person—of all kinds! Throughout the scriptures, Jesus is visiting, talking to, calling upon, and inviting the most surprising people to join with Him. Fishermen, orphan girls, refugees, rookies, farm boys, kids from the other side of the tracks, kids who stutter, kids with a limp, the plain ones, the outsiders.

HE HAS ALWAYS REACHED OUT AND INVITED THE MISFITS.

Over and over we read and hear that gentle and welcoming single-word invitation from Jesus: "Come."

COME FIND PEACE.
COME FIND GRACE. COME FIND
BELONGING. COME FIND HEALING.
COME FIND REST. COME FIND JOY.
COME DOWN. YOU ARE WELCOME HERE.
YOU ARE SPECIFICALLY INVITED HERE.
THERE WOULD BE AN EMPTY
CHAIR WITHOUT YOU, AND
I WOULD NOTICE.

You might not have been invited to the birthday party last week, or to homecoming last year, but the Creator of the world invites you to the table, to the feast, to the Church, to His group of disciples, into His glory, and to His work.

In one of those times when JESUS WAS SITTING DOWN TO LUNCH WITH THE WRONG KIND OF PEOPLE, He was approached by the church leaders who criticized Him for who He was eating with. They wondered why it was always the sinning type and misfits who flocked to Him. Luke wrote in His book (in a different translation than we have in our King James Version of the Bible), "By this time a lot of men and women of doubtful reputation were hanging around Jesus, listening intently. THE PHARISEES AND RELIGION SCHOLARS WERE NOT PLEASED, NOT AT ALL PLEASED. They growled, 'He takes in sinners and eats meals with them, treating them like old friends.'"[6] I love that translation. He wasn't just tolerating the people of doubtful reputation; He was treating them like old friends! Their complaints triggered a set of THREE STORIES FROM THE LORD—about a LOST SHEEP, a LOST COIN, and a LOST SON. I want to focus on the second one—the coin (but all three are fantastic and you can read them in Luke 15). Here is how Jesus explained why He was loving on and having lunch with the kind of people He did. "What woman having ten pieces of silver, if she lose one piece, doth not light a candle, and sweep the house, and seek diligently till she find it? And when she hath found it, she calleth her friends and her neighbours together, saying, Rejoice with me; for I have found the piece which I had lost" (Luke 15:8–9).

Now, there is something wildly illogical about this story. It just doesn't make sense. In Jesus's day, a coin, or denari, was worth about one day's wages. Funny enough,

THE WOMAN ENDS UP SPENDING A WHOLE DAY LOOKING FOR IT

—when she could've been working to earn another one. And when she finds it, she invites over both her friends and her neighbors to have a party to celebrate that she found it. A party that probably cost as much or more than the coin that she actually found. In the end, THE WOMAN SPENDS MORE TIME AND MONEY THAN THE COIN WAS ACTUALLY WORTH. If you went over to her house and she was just sweeping away at nighttime by candlelight, you might say, "Lady, give it up. Just let the coin go. You have nine others. It isn't worth the effort." Or when she invited you to the party you might wonder, why all the fuss over one coin?

It just doesn't make sense.
But neither does the love of Jesus for you.

It is illogical. You won't be able to figure it out.

♡

He does not love us for what we are
or what we can do or have done.
He loves us because we are His.

We are precious in His sight. We might say that we are not worthy of that kind of affection or love. We are just a coin to sit in people's pockets or under couch cushions. But love is not determined by the thing or the person that is loved. It is determined by the one who is loving. The coin did not get to decide what it was worth to the woman. The woman decided what the coin was worth to her.

Worth is determined by what someone is willing to pay for something. And Jesus was willing to die for us.

That is what He thinks we are worth. All people! We don't get to decide that—He does. The Lord has said, "Remember the worth of souls is great in the sight of God; For, behold, the Lord your Redeemer suffered death in the flesh; wherefore he suffered the pain of all men, that all men might repent and come unto him" (D&C 18:10–11).

Jesus doesn't love us and invite us in because it is His duty or responsibility. He isn't just doing His job. HE DOESN'T JUST ACCEPT US OR APPRECIATE US—HE ADORES US! And He proved that to all of us in Gethsemane and on the cross and in the way He lived day to day. This is a love that isn't based on what we have done or who we are; it is a love based on who He is. He is Love personified.

When John ends his biography about the life of Jesus—his job shadowing—he says, "And there are also many other things which Jesus did, the which, if they should be written every one, I suppose that even the world itself could not contain the books that should be written" (John 21:25). Give me these books, I say! Tell me another story of Jesus. Another scene of breathtaking tenderness. Another compassionate detour. I would give anything for another chance to see Him love, help, and save.

Sometimes you might feel like your life is in rags, or that you are so disgusting inside or out, or so different that you need to go to a place where no one else ever goes. You may have been treated unkindly, harshly, or unfairly. You may have sat alone at lunch. You may yearn for love and approval but feel like you are unfit for or unworthy of it. The world can be so cruel.

> **BUT EVEN IF OTHERS HAVE TREATED YOU LIKE YOU WERE DISEASED OR DIRTY OR AN OUTCAST, JESUS WON'T. EVEN IF YOU HAVE TREATED YOURSELF THAT WAY, JESUS DOESN'T. AND HE WISHES SO BADLY THAT YOU WOULDN'T. HE GOES OUT OF HIS WAY TO BE WITH YOU. HE LEADS OUT WITH TENDER, SWEET, GENTLE LOVE. EVERY TIME.**

And so do those who truly follow Him. You can always expect a compassionate touch, embrace, or conversation from Him. He will be **WELCOMING AND KIND** in the thoughts He has for you and the promptings He sends you. He will meet you in the places you are, just as you are. That is who Jesus is. And if we wrote down all the times we see this kind of Jesus in our own stories, I suppose the world couldn't contain the books that would be written.

Each of these stories—all of the stories—answer the question I wear on my bracelet. **WHAT WOULD JESUS DO?** My friend Grace came across someone wearing a really similar bracelet to my WWJD one, but it had different letters: HWLF. When she asked the person about it, she learned about a guy who, like me, had worn a WWJD bracelet for years before finally asking himself—"Wait. What would Jesus do? **WHAT IS THE ANSWER TO THE QUESTION?** I already know. Why do I keep wearing the question instead of wearing the answer?" HWLF.

"He would love first."

That was Jesus's first step in every story. Love. Before coming up with solutions and without judgment, **HIS FIRST MOVE—HIS BEST MOVE—WAS ALWAYS LOVE.** It's the best way to help and the only way to save. At the end of a busy day—a day filled with teaching, and preaching, and healing, Jesus looked at the multitudes of people that lived in a certain city, and Matthew said He was "moved with compassion." There were so many people in need. So many who felt unwanted, unworthy, and unloved. "Then saith he unto his disciples, The harvest truly is plenteous, but the labourers are few." Look, He said. All those people need love. They need a tender touch or a listening ear. And there aren't enough of us to do it. So He asked them a favor: "Pray ye therefore the Lord of the harvest, that he will send forth labourers into his harvest" (Matthew 9:36–37).

Will you pray that the Father sends more to do the work? The work of lifting and encouraging?

I think you who are reading this book are an answer to that prayer. I think He sent you as laborers in His harvest of souls—the kind of people He knew would live and love like Him.

Whatever you choose to do in your life—even if you are a dentist— THE GREATEST THING YOU WILL EVER DO IS TO BE LIKE JESUS. To ask yourself the question WWJD, and live out the answer HWLF.

THE TENDER JESUS

Treats us with kindness and gentleness.
Has a soft heart toward all people.
Always has love as His motive.

6
THE HOPE OF ISRAEL

Just so you know, I come from a baseball family. My grandpa never missed the home opening game for the Houston Astros. He was hopelessly devoted. He passed on that love to all of us. In 2017 when the Astros won the World Series for the first time in franchise history, it very well could've been one of the happiest days of my life. I still tear up a little when I watch the reruns of it. I lived off of that high for months! Last season, my five-year-old son faked sick from school so he could watch game two of the division championship. I didn't know five-year-olds even knew skipping school was a thing. I have never been prouder.

A couple of baseball seasons ago I had some friends playing in the high school state championship tournament. They were underdogs going in, but they looked just good enough and had just enough bite and passion to give all of us the reasonable belief that they could make it all the way to the end. It would be a tough road, but it was possible.

It was the ninth inning in a deciding game, and our team was up to bat. We had a runner on first base and another on third, with only one out. The boy up to bat would be the tying run, and he was a money hitter. WE WERE IN A PRIME SPOT FOR A HERO'S ENDING to the game. The batter batted and had two foul balls that put him at two strikes. We were all on our feet. Palms were sweaty, moms covered their eyes and peeked through cracks in their fingers, whistles echoed through the stands, and half-eaten bowls of nachos were set aside.

INNING	1 2 3 4 5 6 7 8 9
VISITOR	2 0 5 2 0 1 1 0 0
HOME	0 6 0 3 4 0 0 0
BALL 2 STRIKE 2 OUT 0	

A hit here could take them into the semifinals. Most of the team on the field were seniors in high school and had played with each other since Little League. Their dream of making it to the championship game was taking shape. It was destined to be a fairy-tale finish.

In came the pitch, and the runner on first took off, stealing second base. Swing and a miss. Strike three. The batter was out. And then before anyone could even grumble in temporary disappointment, the catcher caught the ball and threw a rocket to second base to tag out the runner as he slid in. Got him. Three outs. Ball game.

I'm not sure if anyone breathed on our side of the field. There was just silent shock. Every mouth hung open. Wait a minute! It's over? Just like that? We couldn't believe it. THiS iSN'T HOW iT iS SUPPOSED TO END. This was their dream! The storybook ending! The excitement dropped like a ride at an amusement park. My mind was yelling for a redo. A do-over. A second chance! But that was it. Game over. The ump called it. He had no compassion. For the love of the game, man! How about one more inning? Why stop at nine? Ten is a more even number anyway. But no such luck. Those were the rules, and the rules won out. All that was left were cheers from the other fans, quiet congratulatory fist bumps, tears brushed quickly and quietly from dusty cheeks, and half-eaten bowls of nachos tossed into the trash. That had been their last chance at the trophy. The game was over, and they left empty-handed.

That is not a happy memory. And if any of you boys read this chapter, I am sorry I brought it up again. But all of us should know that there are some things in life that are like this. Some things you get only one shot at.

IN BASEBALL GAMES, THREE STRIKES AND YOU ARE OUT. THE RULES ARE THE RULES.

But guess what? Even though those boys' state baseball championship chances have run out, THEY ARE ALL STILL TOGETHER PLAYING ON THE SAME TEAM. JUST IN A DIFFERENT FIELD. One that is "white already to harvest" (D&C 4:4). They traded in their jerseys for button-up white shirts and ties and have gone out into the different parts of this world to declare a better story than the one I told you about them. The greatest story of all time—the good news. The best news.

> The story of Jesus. And in that story, there are do-overs. And there are second chances.

Hope never runs out, and "to be continued" is at the bottom of every page.

ONE OF JESUS'S NAMES IS THE HOPE OF ISRAEL.

But who is Israel, and why do they need hope? One of the things those baseball boys are doing out in the world is handing out copies of the Book of Mormon to people. That is a book that was specifically written to give people HOPE IN SECOND CHANCES. To give them HOPE IN JESUS. In the title page of that book, Mormon actually wrote his purpose for including the stories that he did. Let's just have a moment of thanksgiving for Mormon, shall we? The Lord gave Mormon the job of walking into a cave full of a thousand years of history and records by Nephite kings and prophets. He then went through all of it to summarize and handpick the parts that would be most beneficial for us today. What a job! OUT OF ALL THAT HE HAD TO READ THROUGH,

WHY DID HE CHOOSE THE PARTICULAR STORIES AND PASSAGES THAT HE DID? Well, he told us. This is from his own hand:

> This book "is to show unto the remnant of the house of Israel what great things the Lord hath done for their fathers; and that they may know the covenants of the Lord, that they are not cast off forever."

That is purpose number one. The house of Israel were God's chosen and covenant people throughout the history of the earth. They were the ones that He made eternal promises with, and **HE SENT THEM OUT TO BLESS ALL THE NATIONS OF THE WORLD.** Crazy enough, as good as God is, instead of loving Him back and influencing the world, the house of Israel chose other gods and let the world influence them. They turned their back on Him again and again. They rejected His prophets and ignored His love. Israel was known for running away from the Lord and His goodness. That isn't something you want to be known for, by the way.

It should have been **GAME OVER** for the house of Israel. They had their chances! They rejected Him! This is their story all through the books of scripture. One example of it is told in this little book called the book of Hosea in the Old Testament. Hosea was a prophet that the Lord commanded to go and marry a woman who had a sort of bad reputation (see Hosea 1:2). Her name was Gomer (bless her heart!). Hosea did what the Lord asked and married her—name and all. He loved and adored his bride like no other husband had before. She was the apple to his pie. I imagine he wrote her love notes, left little treasures where she could find them, and hurried home every day after work just to see her face again. They had three children together, and it seemed like they were a #couplegoals type of match.

However, Gomer did not return the love that Hosea gave to her. One day when he came home, she wasn't there. She had left. And she didn't just leave, but she left him for someone else. She cheated on him and was gone and back to her old, scandalous ways of life. "I will go after my lovers," she said (Hosea 2:5). Hosea was rejected. Betrayed. This must have broken his heart. Right in two. Of course it did, right? No surprise. What is surprising is what happened next.

Life did not work out for Gomer very well, so she said she wanted to "return to my first husband; for then was it better with me than now" (v. 7).

What do you think Hosea thought when he found out Gomer wanted to come back after things in her new life didn't turn out? What do you think he said to her? What would you say?

I know what I would say. Adios, Gomer. That's what I would say. You left me and the kids, and now that your other lover boys have left you, you want to come back? Nope! But Hosea had a different response. "I will allure her," he said (v. 14). I am going to try and win her love again!

Tragically, Gomer had been sold into slavery for some of the choices she made. *Tough luck* is my first thought. That is the life you chose! But not Hosea. He goes out looking for her. Probably into the worst parts of town. And finally he finds her, broken, enslaved, horrified, and embarrassed, and he "bought her . . . for fifteen pieces of silver, and for an homer of barley, and an half homer of barley" (Hosea 3:2). He buys her back from the slave owners! And then he brings her home with promises of a happy future! "Thou shalt abide for me many days," he said (v. 3).

WHAT DO YOU THINK ABOUT THIS STORY? What would you say if you were texting back and forth with Hosea and all of a sudden he says—"Oh my gosh, I gotta go. Gomer is in trouble." I'll tell you what I would say. Kick. Her. To. The. Curb. That's what I would say. Goodbye, Gomer! Three strikes and you are out. You are a liar and a cheater and you are not welcome here. Once I can probably forgive. Twice maybe. But again and again and again? Nope. Too much.

You might be wondering why such a story is in the Bible. It just seems crazy! But this same story is actually all over the scriptures. Just with different names. Hosea was not writing the book to give marriage or relationship advice, but he wrote it to give a metaphor.

A METAPHOR OF THE LOVE STORY BETWEEN THE LORD AND ISRAEL.

Hosea is the Lord, and Gomer is Israel. **I AM GOMER. YOU ARE GOMER.** The Lord has been so good to me and has loved me despite who I am. And I have cheated on Him with sin. I've turned my back and left Him. Betrayed Him. I have gone off to find other things that make me happy. There have been plenty of times when I have ignored His constant and kind requests and then gotten myself deep in trouble and debt and slavery. And what does He do?

"I will betroth thee unto me for ever; yea, I will betroth thee unto me in righteousness, and in judgment, and in lovingkindness, and in mercies" (Hosea 2:19).

He takes me back again and again. With loving-kindness and mercy.

Now what do you want Hosea to say to Gomer once you realize she is you? "Take her back! She didn't mean to! Give her another chance!" And that is exactly what the Lord does. This is the story of the people of Israel and their God.

This is what that second half of the line from the title page of the Book of Mormon means. Another reason for that book was to remind the people about the "covenants of the Lord, that they were not cast off forever." It was to show that EVEN THOUGH ISRAEL (OR WE) HAD CONTINUED TO REJECT THE LORD, THE LORD WOULD NOT REJECT ISRAEL. He is their merciful God. He is their hope for a better life. Their hope for forgiveness. The Hope of Israel.

"They will deny me; nevertheless, I will be merciful unto them, saith the Lord God, if they will repent and come unto me; for mine arm is lengthened out all the day long" (2 Nephi 28:32).

CAN WE REALLY HAVE A GOD THAT IS THIS GOOD? When Enos, one of the Book of Mormon prophets, was out on a hunting trip, he prayed to the Lord and wrestled internally with something day and night. Perhaps it was for forgiveness. Perhaps he was having a Gomer moment and pleading to come back. As he was out kneeling in the woods, he said a voice came to him and said, "Enos, thy sins are forgiven thee, and thou shalt be blessed" (Enos 1:5).

We don't know what Enos's life was like before, but he seemed to be overwhelmed with the mercy he felt and asked the Lord, "HOW iS iT DONE?" Every time I read that, I think about the times I have asked the Lord similar questions. How is this possible? How can You take me back, Lord? How could You afford to give me one more chance? I've done so much wrong. I've wandered and sold myself into sin. My chances are up.

And then this answer came to Enos:

"BECAUSE OF THY FAITH IN CHRIST"
(ENOS 1:8).

It is not because of you, Enos; it is because of Him.

Our sins prevent us from being able to live forever in the presence of God, for "no unclean thing can dwell with God" (1 Nephi 10:21). In the book of Romans, Paul tells us that the wage of our sin, or the result of our sin, is death (see Romans 6:23). Sin has both temporal and eternal consequences that cannot be ignored. They can't just be brushed under the rug or forgotten about. If you drop your ice cream on someone or forget someone's birthday or fall and break someone's spikeball net (sorry, bud!), most people just respond with a "hey, no biggie." But God cannot do this because of His eternal laws. The law of justice insists that a sin must be met with a punishment. Every time. No second chances with the law. The prophet Alma had a son who got caught up in some heavy sin. Like father, like son, some might say. Alma was trying to help his son understand how serious of a situation sin is when he told him, "But there is a law given, and a punishment affixed, and a repentance granted; which repentance, mercy claimeth; otherwise, justice claimeth the creature and executeth the law, and the law inflicteth the punishment; if not so, the works of justice would be destroyed, and God would cease to be God" (Alma 42:22).

There are two things in Alma's one-on-one sermon to his boy Corianton I want y'all to catch. The first is what we were just saying. SiN CAN'T BE iGNORED. The law of justice cannot be broken or God would cease to be God. And justice and punishment will claim those who sin. Just like Gomer—sold into slavery. The sins have to be answered for. But Alma was a good dad and was trying to breathe hope into his son. There was also a much more encouraging part of that verse. Did you see it?

●━•━•━•━●━•━•━•━●━•━•━•━•●━•━

THE FACT THAT MERCY CAN CLAIM YOU INSTEAD OF JUSTICE. OR, BETTER SAID—JESUS CAN CLAIM YOU INSTEAD OF JUSTICE. BECAUSE HE SUFFERED AND DIED FOR OUR SINS, HE IS ABLE TO FORGIVE US OF THOSE SINS AND TAKE US BACK. WE CAN HAVE HOPE!

●━•━•━•━●━•━•━•━●━•━•━•━●━•━

The law of justice has been answered by Him, the ransom has been paid, and now He has the right to claim us as His. And He does it with open arms. But we are the ones who have to walk back to Him. He will persuade us, but He will not force us to return. This has been the case from the very beginning.

In the book of Genesis, we read a story about Adam and Eve. Now, before I tell you the story, you should know that there are two ways to read the story of Adam and Eve. One of the ways to read it is symbolically—to pretend that Adam and Eve represent all people and eating the fruit is a symbol of committing sin. In real life, leaving the Garden of Eden was actually a good thing! We celebrate their decision. But right now, we are looking at the story symbolically.

In the beginning book of Genesis, God planted an orchard for Adam and Eve and gave them hundreds of trees to eat fruit from. ALL THE FRUIT YOU COULD EVER DREAM OF. Peach trees, apple trees, pear trees, and strawberry trees. I don't know if strawberry trees are a thing, but they should be! God was so, so good to them! But you may remember that Adam and Eve went and ate from the one tree that was forbidden. They walked away from Him and disobeyed His counsel. Maybe, like Gomer, they thought the other tree was better than what God was giving them. Not long after they ate the fruit, they heard the voice of the Lord coming. And do you know what they did next? They ran and hid. It is kind of funny that they thought they could actually hide from God. They were literally crouching behind a tree that HE created. They not only hid, but they tried to cover themselves with fig leaves, too. Why would they do that? What were they feeling? Guilt? Shame? Regret? The next part is classic. The Lord asked Adam, "Where art thou?" (Genesis 3:8) Don't you love that? THE LORD KNOWS EXACTLY WHERE ADAM IS, but He still calls out to him. I love the way the book of Moses translates that same question. Adam, "Where goest thou?" (Moses 4:15). Where are you going? What are you doing? Why are you running from the only person who can actually help you? What lie did the old devil tell you that made you think you would want to run and hide in shame?

We all commit sin and make mistakes and wish we hadn't. But we do. Paul, the professional-sinner-turned-Apostle, testified that

"All [including him] have sinned, and come short of the glory of God" (Romans 3:23). And when we do sin, we often copy what Adam and Eve did and try to cover it up or run from it—or worse, run from our only Hope, Jesus. The only One who can heal and fix it.

THE TRUTH IS, WE CANNOT HIDE FROM THE LORD, BUT WE DON'T NEED TO HIDE FROM THE LORD.

Whatever lie Satan has told you about Him, let me show you a story of the real Jesus. A Jesus you would never run from. This story is in John 8.

One day, He was in the temple with faithful disciples when a commotion was heard near the entryway. A crowd of people gathered as a woman was dragged in to where the Lord was and thrown in front of Him. The people who had brought the woman to Jesus said, "Master, this woman was taken in adultery, in the very act. Now . . . the law commanded us, that such should be stoned: but what sayest thou?" (John 8:4–5). Did you catch that? THE LAW SAYS SHE iS TOAST.

Can you even imagine this scene? Do we dare wonder what this woman was feeling? Imagine you are sitting in sacrament meeting and all of a sudden the doors bang open and a mob of people come dragging in Sister So-and-So up to the pulpit to announce why she was not at church and the sins she was committing that morning. The woman from this story in John was guilty of a very serious sin, and I bet the last place she wanted to be was in the temple in front of Jesus and her friends having her sins announced to everyone who could hear. Everyone must have turned to Jesus and listened to see how He would handle the situation. As they watched, Jesus did something sort of bizarre. He didn't say anything, but stooped down to the ground and started writing in the dust and sand "as though he heard them not" (John 8:6). What was He doing?! How weird! Why wasn't He answering? Everyone must have been wide-eyed and totally confused. They asked Him a question, and He just seemed to be coloring in the sand!

The atmosphere had been wild and frenzied, and He slowed it down by calmly running His finger through the dirt. HiS POSTURE SPOKE PEACE iNTO THE MADNESS. When they asked again, Jesus gave His famous response: "He that is without sin among you, let him first cast a stone at her" (John 8:7). He then stooped down again to write more. As people felt convicted of their own sins, one by one they left them alone. They left her alone.

I don't think anyone will know what Jesus wrote on the ground of the temple that day. If it had been important, John probably would have mentioned it. But I don't think what He wrote was the point. WHEN THE WOMAN CAME iN, ALL EYES WERE ON HER. Judgments, whispers, condemnations, and gasps. But as He stooped down in the middle of the crowd and silently wrote on the ground, WHERE DO YOU THiNK THE PEOPLE STARTED LOOKiNG? I always imagine they looked right at Him. Now the whispers were about Him. And by consequence, where did they stop looking? And who did they stop gasping about? In that moment, I picture His action taking all of the attention and scorn off of the woman and moving it onto Him. Jesus absorbed every ounce of the toxic and poisonous spirit those men had been firing at the woman. That is what He is like. And then, in His perfect way, He excused all of the onlookers until it was just the two of them. No accusers. No stones. Just them. He handled the most embarrassing situation so gently. We wish we had more of the conversation they had when the people left. It definitely included the charge to go home and "sin no more"—the charge to change and repent and live a life of purity. But iT ALSO iNCLUDED A SECOND CHANCE. Look around, He said. Where are your accusers? Is there anyone left? Is anyone condemning you to death?

No, Lord. No one is.

"Neither do I condemn thee" (John 8:10–11).

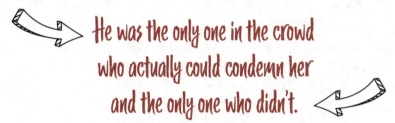

He was the only one in the crowd who actually could condemn her and the only one who didn't.

And He is also the only one in the room who would take her condemnation upon Himself. A condemnation that would bring about His death. Oh, I don't know everything they talked about, but in the end, I like to think there was also an invitation to return to the temple another day, when she was ready, under different circumstances.

That is the Jesus that Adam and Eve were running from. Do you think that if they had known His character they would've hidden? I don't think so.

THAT IS THE SAME TENDERNESS YOU CAN EXPECT WHEN YOU REPENT AND RETURN TO YOUR SAVIOR.

It is the same kind of tenderness you should receive and expect from your parents and bishop when you go to them for help and support in that process. Even if this is the one hundredth time you have gone.

Jesus has said, "Yea, and as often as my people repent will I forgive them their trespasses against me" (Mosiah 26:30).

The story of the people of Israel is a story of God reaching out again and again to give them another chance. And that is our story. THERE IS NEVER A TIME WHEN WE ARE WITHOUT HOPE. There may be days you are tempted to just run and hide. To think that you are done for. To think that God could never forgive you again. Days you feel like you are all out of chances and hope. But hope is not just a feeling; it is a person. There will always be hope for Israel because of the Hope of Israel.

> BECAUSE OF HIM, OUR SINS DO NOT NEED TO BE OUR STORY. THEY DO NOT NEED TO DEFINE US. JUSTICE DOES NOT NEED TO CLAIM US. HE IS ABLE TO GIVE US SECOND CHANCES, AND HE IS BEGGING US TO TAKE THEM.

He doesn't stand over us with a rock in His hand; He is down in the dirt with us. On our level. Ready to raise us up to begin a new life again and again.

Don't get me wrong. There are definite consequences for our decisions, and turning from sin can be a long and difficult process. I once read that it is "better to prepare and prevent than it is to repair and repent."[7] That is very, very, very true. A lot of heartache can be avoided by avoiding sin. It can be addicting, overwhelming, and can cause you to feel hopeless and depressed. However, far too many of us define ourselves by the sins we have committed and the mistakes we have made. We treat them like they are permanent stamps on our passport through life. The Lord knows we have and will make mistakes. We are all sinners. Every one of us. But OUR CHANCES TO RETURN AND BE FORGIVEN NEVER RUN OUT. We forget sometimes that His grace is wider than the sum of all our sins. Listen to His promise:

"BEHOLD, HE WHO HAS REPENTED OF HIS SINS, THE SAME IS FORGIVEN, AND I, THE LORD, REMEMBER THEM NO MORE" (D&C 58:42).

One time in my Sunday School class growing up, my teacher brought in a big long wooden board with nails sticking out of it. He also had a hammer that he used to pull the nails out. He told us our sins were like the nails and the hammer was a symbol for the Savior, who could pull them out of us. The object lesson seemed nice, but I was always bothered by it because of the holes that were left in the board. Will there always be lasting consequences? Will my record always be marked?

President Boyd K. Packer taught, "Our spirits are damaged when we make mistakes and commit sins. But unlike the case of our mortal bodies, when the repentance process is complete, NO SCARS REMAIN because of the Atonement of Jesus Christ."[8]

Odds are that we will remember our sins even if God does not hold us accountable for them anymore. For a lot of our sins, there are lasting consequences. A lot of addiction, for example, takes time to fully overcome—maybe someone's whole life. When we repent, we feel a surge of hope and forgiveness and peace, but that does not mean our journey of being changed and made pure is over. That's a longer journey.

> When the Lord rescued the children of Israel from slavery in Egypt, He did it overnight. He opened an ocean for them. But getting them to the promised land took forty years.

Or perhaps we can say that getting them ready for the promised land took forty years. It did not take long to get the children of Israel out of Egypt, but it took some time to get Egypt out of them. And so it is with our sins.

> The Savior can forgive them immediately. But the process of changing our hearts takes some time.

But the good news is that you can change and you can take that journey even if you have made those mistakes. It is probably most accurate to describe ourselves in present progressive. Sorry to bring English class into this, but present progressive means currently, ongoing. Our sins are in the past, but our path to become holy is present and ongoing—healing and changing and progressing. We will be wounded and a work in progress and messy our whole lives. AND THAT IS PERFECTLY OKAY. The direction we are facing is more important than the location we are at on the journey.

His love never expires,
and His grace is BIGGER and WIDER than all of our sin.

He is far more patient with us than we are with ourselves. Joseph Smith learned from James that He "giveth to all men liberally" (James 1:5), and that includes chances. There will never be a point of no return with Him. Opportunities to change will never run out. He is not a three-strikes-you're-out God.

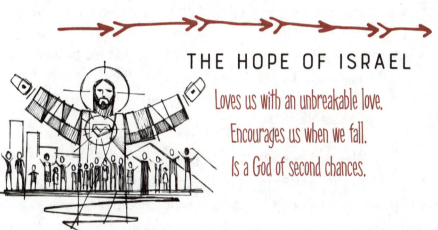

THE HOPE OF ISRAEL

Loves us with an unbreakable love.
Encourages us when we fall.
Is a God of second chances.

1

THE UNFAILING DELIVERER

For some reason, one of my sons was always fascinated by pictures of Jesus on the cross. He was actually fascinated by any of the gospel pictures and videos that had pain or suffering or death in them. Abinadi in the fire, Alma and Amulek's prison experience, and the "Mormon Message" with the scorpion that stings the kid's foot were his favorites (should I be concerned?). One day, I noticed him looking worriedly at a Crucifixion painting. I watched him stare at it for a while, and then he started to softly touch Jesus's hands and feet in the spots where they were nailed to the cross. He did that for a little bit and then looked up at me and said in the cutest little-boy voice,

"Why did Jesus have to get the spikes?"

My wife was sitting right by us and overheard the question. She looked up, and I looked over at her. She nodded at me in a way to say that it was my turn to answer. He was so young, and I wasn't quite sure how to explain it, so I said the first thing that popped into my head: "To satisfy the infinite and eternal demands of justice." Obviously my son had no clue what that meant (I don't think I knew entirely what that meant). He looked at me with a confused face, and Jenny looked at me with the "try again" face.

Then I remembered Jacob from the Book of Mormon and his sermon on monsters.

Do you remember that part?

"O the greatness of the mercy of our God, the Holy One of Israel! For he delivereth his saints from that awful monster the devil, and death, and hell.... For the atonement satisfieth the demands of his justice ... they are delivered from that awful monster, death and hell"

(2 Nephi 9:19, 26).

So I set it up. I said, "Pretend that Mom is heaven." (Not too hard to do!) "I want you to walk to her." Right when my son started to go, I grabbed him and held on to him really tight. He tried to wiggle out but he couldn't (I'm a pretty strong dude). I told him that there were MONSTERS NAMED "THE DEVIL AND DEATH AND HELL" who were holding on to him and wouldn't let go. I asked him if he wanted to be free from the monsters, and of course he said yes.

"Well, you can't," I told him. "They are too big and too strong to get away from on your own.

But you have a hero who can save you from them. Someone stronger than the monsters. That hero is Jesus Christ.

And when He died on the cross and was resurrected on Easter, He got the power to defeat the monsters and set you free."

I then gave my best monster-dying groan and collapsed to the ground as my son went running over to Jenny.

As he gets older, I will need to explain to him more of the story and some of the truths surrounding the Atonement of Christ, but for that day and for the rest of his life, the truth I wanted him and all my kids to know is that they have a hero.

A DELIVERER.

The Fall of Adam and Eve took us all out of the presence of God. This is called spiritual death. We can't make it back on our own. We are powerless. We can't fly or pierce the veil. We are stuck—away and out of God's heavenly home where we belong. But it gets worse.

The Fall also brought physical death into the world. Often people think about death as a good thing, because they think it will take them back into the presence of God. But that isn't true.

THE RESURRECTION TAKES YOU BACK. NOT DEATH.

Without the Resurrection, death would be permanent and final. Jacob in his monster sermon even said that without "an infinite atonement . . . , this flesh must have laid down to rot and to crumble to its mother earth, to rise no more. . . . . And our spirits must have become . . . devils, angels to a devil, to be shut out from the presence of our God, and to remain with the father of lies, in misery, like unto himself" (2 Nephi 9:7, 9).

Without someone to rescue us, our bodies would rot in the ground and our spirits would be cast out of God's presence forever and ever—leaving us to live with and become like the devil. We would be in tremendous amounts of trouble.

No wonder the prophet Abinadi said to King Noah, "Thus all mankind were lost; and behold, they would have been endlessly lost were it not that God redeemed his people from their lost and fallen state" (Mosiah 16:4).

The most hopeful words in that verse from Abinadi are "WERE iT NOT." They are a Book of Mormon way of saying "unless." Unless someone was ABLE AND WiLLiNG to rescue us, save us, and deliver us, then we were lost forever.

The good news is that someone was willing and able. And His name is Jesus, the Deliverer.

The effects and consequences of the Fall are not our fault, but they are our problem. Just because we didn't bring about the Fall doesn't mean we don't inherit the problems of it. The second article of faith says that "men will be punished for their own sins, and not for Adam's transgression." Adam's transgression is what brought about the Fall. If I were allowed to add something to that particular article of faith, I would add in a "you're welcome" at the end. We will not be punished for Adam's transgression, but someone took the punishment and effects of it for us. Being set loose from the effects of spiritual death and physical death was a free gift to us, BUT IT WAS NOT FREE. When I was younger, I went on a lot of family vacations that I thought were free. I was unaware of the hours and hours of sacrifice and work that my parents had had to endure so that they could give me that gift. Yes, they were free to me—but not to them. There was a cost. And that is true about our redemption, too.

IT COST JESUS HIS LIFE TO DELIVER US.

The prophet Samuel from the Book of Mormon understood this and was so determined for everyone else to know it that he shimmied up a wall and stood in a hailstorm of stones and arrows to deliver the message that the Lord put into his heart (if you want to read it for yourself, go to Helaman chapters 13–15). As someone terrified of heights (and, I suppose, arrows flying at my face too), I have always felt extra grateful for the words Samuel shared. He must have felt it was worth the risk to speak these words: "For behold, [Jesus] surely must die that salvation may come; . . . for all mankind, by the fall of Adam being cut off from the presence of the Lord, are considered as dead, both as to things temporal and to things spiritual.

BUT BEHOLD, THE RESURRECTION OF CHRIST REDEEMETH MANKIND, YEA, EVEN ALL MANKIND, AND BRINGETH THEM BACK INTO THE PRESENCE OF THE LORD" (HELAMAN 14:15–17).

It is only through His death and Resurrection that we can be redeemed, delivered, and taken back into the presence of the Lord.

ONCE WE ARE BROUGHT BACK INTO HIS PRESENCE, THE QUESTION BECOMES WHETHER WE WILL STAY THERE OR NOT. THAT IS UP TO US.

Like we talked about in the last chapter, our sins, yet another monster, prevent us from staying and living in the presence of God.

Sin has always been the source of so much heartache and so many problems in the world. It breaks up families, starts world wars, and has the eventual consequence of eternal separation from our God. It is a problem we get ourselves into and have no power to get out of. WE CANNOT SAVE OURSELVES FROM OUR SINS. We cannot pay for one millionth of one percent of any of our sins. WE MUST BE DELIVERED AND SAVED FROM OUR SINS BY AN "INFINITE AND ETERNAL SACRIFICE" (Alma 34:10). For some reason that I don't know, the rescue from sin required the sacrifice and life of a sinless God. Infinite and eternal. It's the only way. HE IS THE ONLY WAY.

Jesus once told His disciples a little story to teach them about how expensive this saving actually is. You can read it in Matthew 18. It is about a man who owed his lord or master ten thousand talents. It is hard to convert ancient money perfectly to modern amounts, but many Bible scholars think that ten thousand talents would be around $1 billion or more. That is a crazy amount of zeroes! It was an ASTRONOMICAL AMOUNT that NO ONE in that time would ever be able to pay back—especially a servant working a minimum-wage job. It would take him lifetimes upon lifetimes to repay the money—over ten thousand years! (I did the math.) The only other option was for all the man's things to be taken away and for him and his family to be sold into slavery for the rest of their lives. The servant begged his master to show him mercy and give him time to repay the money, but it was a ridiculous request. The master knew it, and the servant knew it too. There was no way. It would have been like trying to buy the island of Jamaica with the money from a lemonade stand in the middle of winter. Impossible. And then the Savior gave this line in the parable (the best line, in my opinion):

> "Then the lord of that servant was
> moved with compassion, and loosed him,
> and forgave him the debt" (Matthew 18:27).

All of it. Forgiven. Just one zero left.

That is not the end of the parable, but among other lessons, Jesus was trying to show His role as Savior. A debt is a problem that we get ourselves into. In the parable, the debt can represent the

hole we dig ourselves into with our own sins. With our own dumbness or forgetfulness or even rebellion or apathy. Those sins would be and are as much as a $1 billion debt on a servant's salary. Impossible to get free of on our own. Our only option would be to be sold off as a slave forever.

WE NEED A SAVIOR—SOMEONE CAPABLE OF PAYING BACK THE CASH AND RELEASING US FROM THE BONDAGE WE COULDN'T GET OUT OF IN A THOUSAND LIFETIMES. AND WE HAVE ONE! A WILLING AND FORGIVING SAVIOR IN JESUS.

There is an aspect of this parable that is so important to realize. I didn't catch it myself for years. The debt was forgiven, but it was not just brushed under the rug. IT DIDN'T JUST DISAPPEAR. For any forgiven debt, someone has to bear the weight and cost of it. If I took a hundred dollars from you and then lost it, what are our options? You either make me pay it back somehow (no matter how long it takes) or you forgive it. But if you forgive it, that means that you have now lost it. You have to swallow the cost of it. In this parable, it is the master who swallows the cost in order to forgive the debt. All of that money the lord forgave in the parable—the ten thousand talents—was an amount that even most kings did not have in those days.[9] That means that in the parable, it would have most likely bankrupted the master in order to release the servant. It was not just pocket change.

HE WOULD HAVE TO GIVE UP HIS FORTUNE IN ORDER TO FORGIVE.

Jesus was capable of delivering us because He was the Son of God. But this does not mean that it was easy or cheap. Quite the opposite, in fact. President Boyd K. Packer once said, "He, by choice, ACCEPTED THE PENALTY iN BEHALF Of ALL MANKiND for the sum total of all wickedness . . . ; for brutality, immorality, perversion, for corruption; for addiction; for the killings and torture and terror—all of it that ever had been or that ever would be enacted upon this earth. In so choosing HE FACED THE AWESOME POWER Of THE EViL ONE, who was not confined to flesh nor subject to mortal pain."[10] THAT WAS THE GREAT COST THAT JESUS PAiD TO RESCUE US FROM OUR SiNS.

Let's talk about one more monster that Jesus Christ delivers us from. Part of the impact of the Fall of Adam and Eve is that we live here on earth in a fallen condition. Mortality brings so many problems with it. There is sickness, tragedy, natural disaster, and the sin of others. People you know will suffer because of diseases. Others will have accidents that leave them crippled or paralyzed for life. And even more others are born with and into conditions that are so heavy to carry. Homes are lost to fires and floods, and a smooth-sailing life can become rough, choppy seawaters overnight. And because we are fallen, natural-man people in a fallen world, a lot of the hard parts of life come from each other. We have caused way more tears for each other than all the hurricanes and cancer cells ever did.

Living in this mortal world is necessary for us to grow and progress and become like our Heavenly Parents. Life can be a great teacher and these experiences strengthen us and refine our hearts, but,

Oh man, it can be a whirlwind.

Compared to eternity, our life on earth is not very long, but it sure seems like a whole lot of stuff is squeezed into a whole little bit of time. Elder Neal A. Maxwell, who knew his share of trouble with mortality, said our life in the end will seem so short—like being dropped off by a parent for a single day of school. But then he followed that up with, "But what a day!"[11]

> Jesus came to not only save us from the Fall, sin, and death, but to also save us from those parts of life that can be so unfair.

Do you remember the story Jesus told about the man who comes down from Jerusalem to Jericho and gets attacked? We call it the story of the good Samaritan. You can read it in Luke 10. On this man's trip, he is headed down to Jericho and is jumped by these robbers who steal his clothes and cash, rough him up real good, and leave him half dead on the side of the road (see Luke 10:30). As he lies there broken and bloody, he is passed by a priest on one side of him and a Levite temple worker on the other side. Who can blame them for going right on by? IT WAS A DANGEROUS ROAD, after all. What if the thieves were still around? And they were probably busy with church callings or other things. So they leave him there for dead. But then a Samaritan comes. And if you were hearing this story back in Jesus's day, you would expect the Samaritan to pass by, because Samaritans and Jews didn't get along. They were from rival teams. Enemies in some circles. "But [he] . . . came where he was: and when he saw him, HE HAD COMPASSION ON HIM, and went to him, and bound up his wounds, pouring in oil and wine, and set him on his own beast, and brought him to an inn, and TOOK CARE OF HIM " (vv. 33–34). I love this parable so much and have read it so many times, the page is literally torn out of the seam of my Bible from being turned so many times.

Many of the early Christian writers considered this parable to not only be about being kind and helpful to others in need but to also be a story about the redeeming and delivering Jesus.[12] Jerusalem is up on a mountaintop high above sea level, and Jericho is by the Dead Sea in one of the lowest spots on earth. Think symbolically, y'all—this could be a story about a MAN COMING FROM A HIGHER PLACE (a place like heaven) down to a lower one (like earth). And while he is here TRAVELING THE ROAD OF LIFE, he falls among thugs who rob him and hurt him and leave him for dead. Just like us. We have come down from heaven for this journey in a lower place. And while we are here, all of us will be robbed unfairly. We will be robbed of opportunities, peace of mind, safety, and other precious possessions. It will come unexpectedly, unfairly, and undeservedly. So many of us will be hurt and beaten by others and by life circumstances in unthinkable ways. We will be accused and penalized for things we did not do. Things that are out of our control. In some cases, it will be just minor, but at other times we may feel like we are half dead, lying on the side of the road. And there will be many who will come upon us, some of them even church folk, and will not or most likely cannot help us and end up passing us by on the other side.

BUT WE HAVE A SAMARITAN WHO WILL COME.

Samaritans were part Jewish and part foreigner, just like Jesus is part God and part mortal. The good Samaritan comes to where we are—on purpose—and wraps up our wounds, pours in His own healing oil and wine (oil and wine were both symbols for Jesus's Atonement), and carries us to places of safety to watch over us through the night as we heal. He knows how roughed up we will be in this life. He knows our bones will bruise and our hearts will break. He knows our weaknesses, our temptations, and our trials. He knows exactly how each of us feels in every situation.

No one else may even notice. But He does.

You might feel overlooked by everyone else, but you are being looked over by God.

Everything unfair about this life will be made up to us eventually and unconditionally because of the mercy, goodness, and loving-kindness of Jesus Christ. He will personally pour in the healing oil, personally wrap up your wounds, and personally carry you to places of safety.

The Bible Dictionary describes *grace,* in part, as a "DIVINE MEANS OF HELP OR STRENGTH, GIVEN THROUGH THE BOUNTEOUS MERCY AND LOVE OF JESUS CHRIST." Understood best, grace is not a thing—iT iS A PERSON. It is Grace that delivers us from death, sin, and the Fall, but it is also Grace that strengthens us, heals us, and gives us the means to make it through some of the heavy and hard trials of this life.

There will probably be burdens and problems and scars that you will have your entire life. That will be part of mortality. IT WILL BE A BATTLE UNTIL THE END. BUT HE WILL GIVE YOU THE STRENGTH TO ENDURE iT. There is a scripture that I hear a lot, but it is usually only half quoted. It is from a letter that Paul wrote to the Saints living in Corinth. The first part says, "There hath no temptation taken you but such as is common to man: but God is faithful, who will not suffer you to be tempted above that ye are able." This is where I hear a lot of people end. They say something along the lines of—see! God will not let things into your life that you can't handle. But that isn't true. The verse isn't over. Keep reading, folks! The second half says, "But will WITH THE TEMPTATION ALSO MAKE A WAY TO ESCAPE, that ye may be able to bear it" (1 Corinthians 10:13). There *will* be life troubles you cannot handle. If you could handle them all on your own, you wouldn't need a Deliverer. He comes to give strength and grace and eventually escape.

He has said, "Fear not: for I have redeemed thee, I have called thee by thy name; thou art mine. When thou passest through the waters, I will be with thee; and through the rivers, they shall not overflow thee: when thou walkest through the fire, thou shalt not be burned; neither shall the flame kindle upon thee. For I am the Lord thy God, the Holy One of Israel, thy Saviour: . . . thou wast precious in my sight, thou hast been honourable, and I have loved thee: . . . Fear not: for I am with thee" (Isaiah 43:1–5). It has always been beautiful to me that it is a wounded Christ who comes to be with us and eventually deliver us.

> WE WORSHIP A REDEEMER WHO WAS REJECTED. A SAVIOR WHO WAS SLAIN. A DELIVERER WHO WAS DISGRACED. A BELOVED FRIEND WHO WAS BETRAYED. AND A LEADER WHO KNOWS LONELINESS.

He comes with His own scars in His hands, feet, and side. Scars that are signs that He is able and willing to heal. For those problems we carry our whole life, Jesus promises to one day "wipe away all tears from [our] eyes" (Revelation 21:4). IN THE END, and perhaps only in the end, EVERYTHING WILL BE MADE RIGHT. Everything will be made up to you.

All of this is possible—the deliverance from all of these monsters—because of Jesus Christ.

Somehow His suffering in the Garden of Gethsemane, His Crucifixion on the cross, and His Resurrection on Easter morning and the way He lived and loved brought this about. THERE IS A LOT WE DO NOT UNDERSTAND about all of this, and we will get to spend the rest of our lives studying and thinking about it. However, THERE ARE SOME TRUTHS THAT WE DO KNOW ABOUT IT, AND THEY ARE TRUTHS WORTH TALKING ABOUT. In fact, one of those truths, spoken by Lehi more than two thousand years ago, is a scripture that inspired me to serve a mission: "Wherefore, how great the importance to make these things known unto the inhabitants of the earth, that they may know that there is no flesh that can dwell in the presence of God, save it be through the merits, and mercy, and grace of the Holy Messiah" (2 Nephi 2:8).

What we do know is this:

WE WERE IN NEED OF RESCUE. AND JESUS CAME TO THAT RESCUE.

However we try to explain it to people, as long as it leads us to love and adore Him, we are explaining it right.

All throughout scripture there are stories of Jesus delivering people. Blind people were delivered from darkness, the deaf were able to hear again, and dead people were even brought back to life. Jesus stopped the rains, gave strength to armies, calmed the wild seas, and multiplied bread and fishes. Each of these stories is in the scriptures to teach us that HE IS ABLE TO SOLVE ANY PROBLEM WE EVER EXPERIENCE—NO MATTER WHOSE FAULT IT IS. That is what He came to do. To save, rescue, and deliver us from death, the Fall, our sins, and the unfair things about this life, and then change us and exalt us into something more. Something divine. Our Heavenly Father knew we would be in trouble down here, so He created a plan to rescue us from all that trouble. He had a plan to save us—a plan of salvation. And that plan was Jesus. Sometimes when referring to the plan of salvation we draw circles. But I've stopped doing that. I have started drawing a cross to represent God's plan. Circles didn't save us. Jesus did. He was and is and will always be the plan of salvation.

 On the coat of arms of the city of Belfast, Ireland, is the Latin phrase "*Pro tanto quid retirbuamus*," or, translated into English, "WHAT SHALL I GIVE IN RETURN FOR SO MUCH GIVEN TO ME?" That is a question I think about every time I hear stories about our Deliverer.

Imagine one last parable. Once there was a little girl who was with her family at the Grand Canyon. While everyone was busy admiring the amazing views and taking a few pictures, the little girl crawled under the guardrail and fell over the edge. As people screamed and scrambled to look over, they noticed that there was

a rock ledge that stuck out about ten to twenty feet down that the little girl had miraculously landed on. However, it didn't take away the fear. The ledge was not very wide, and the girl was not very good on her wobbly feet. Beyond the little ledge was the several-hundred-feet drop to the bottom and certain death. Almost instinctively, a teenage boy who was there, who was also a rock climber, hopped over the guardrail and scaled down the rocks to the little ledge. When he got there he took the little girl, wrapped her up in his arms, and held her in a tight, safe embrace until rescue teams could arrive.

If you were the parents of that girl, what would you say to the boy when he got back up over the ledge? What could you possibly do to thank him? New climbing gear for Christmas? A gift card? Nope. YOU JUST NEVER FORGET HIM.[13]

What could we possibly do to repay Him for what He has done? Nothing. We could never repay Him—not in ten thousand lifetimes. But WE CAN REMEMBER HIM AND HONOR HIM AND LOVE HIM for the price He paid. We could do that forever and ever. And I plan on it. But even if we did forget, He would never forget us. Not after everything He has been through for you. He will always deliver you. He already has. From debts, from monsters, from robbers, from anything and everything.

THE UNFAILING DELIVERER

Gave His life to be your Rescuer and Redeemer.
Will strengthen you and provide escape.
Is bigger than any of your problems—
no matter whose fault they are.

THE LAMB OF GOD

I have always loved a good underdog story. They make the best movies, the best auditions on *The Voice*, and the best ESPN *30 for 30*s. When I am done watching them, I feel like I can do anything. We have already mentioned this, but it seems like God loves the same types of stories. Shepherd heroes. Teenage prophets. Orphan princesses.

The scriptures are filled with underdog stories and unexpected heroes and endings.

One of my favorites is in the book of Revelation at the end of the New Testament. If you ever get sleepy reading scripture, just open up Revelation. It will wake you right up. It is filled with sea monsters, animals with wings and tons of eyeballs, a mysterious book that cannot be opened, and a wild woman who rides on the back of a beast leaving destruction in her path.

One of the creepiest creatures from the book is a giant, red, seven-headed dragon with horns topped with crowns on its head. He seems to be the ringleader for the bad guys. It whips its tail up into the stars and snatches a third of them and thrusts them out of the heavens as it chases a pregnant woman into the woods—determined to eat her unborn child.[14] Yowzas! One of the major themes from the book of Revelation is about a WAR BETWEEN GOOD AND EVIL. A quest for victory that seems at times to be heavily favored on the dark side—especially with the red dragon at the lead.

But the good guys have a war leader too. You are first introduced to Him in the beginning of the book when the writer comes across a problem too big for him. He cries in defeat and fear. Then, an angel reassures him by announcing their hope:

"WEEP NOT: BEHOLD THE LION OF THE TRIBE OF JUDAH . . . HATH PREVAILED" (REVELATION 5:5).

In my mind, I see John lift his head to look and see his champion—the one who will prevail over the problems, the monsters, the beasts, and the dragon. If I were filming a movie of it, I would have the doorway fill with a smoky mist and play dramatic music to build up the suspense and drama of the HERO'S BIG ENTRANCE. You would hear the footsteps and see the shadow cast into the room as he approached. And then, through the doorway, he appears. The music would stop, the camera would zoom in, and the hero would let out a *baaaaa*. It's a lamb. Can you picture the look of disappointment on everyone's faces? A LAMB?? "I thought you said the Lion of the tribe of Judah," he might say. HOW IS A LAMB GOING TO WIN THE DAY? But that is the hero John presents in the battle story of the book of Revelation. And it is a hero who wins.

THE LAMB OF GOD IS A COMMON NAME AND TITLE FOR JESUS CHRIST.

It is one that the people of the New Testament times were very familiar with. When John the Baptist wanted to let his followers know exactly who Jesus was, he introduced Him as the Lamb of God (see John 1:36). Why would he pick this name? And why did the other John depict Him in the middle of war in the book of Revelation as a barnyard animal? WHY NOT SOMETHING SCARY OR STRONG OR POWERFUL?

As I thought about these questions, I started to think about all the times that a lamb is used throughout the scriptures and what they teach us about Jesus Christ. As I made my list, I started to realize that the lamb shows up everywhere. It starts in the book of Genesis and weaves all the way through until the last book of Revelation. In fact, you could almost nickname the whole Bible as "The Story of the Lamb." Let me share a few of those stories with you to help you understand why John may have chosen this particular name and what it means for us.

When Adam and Eve were cast out of the Garden of Eden for eating the forbidden fruit, they were devastated. They had walked and talked with God in that beautiful place, and now they were out in the lonely and dreary world filled with thorns and weeds and wild things. THEY YEARNED TO BE BACK IN GOD'S PRESENCE and surely begged how it could be possible. How could they return? In answer, God gave them a peculiar commandment to "offer the firstlings of their flocks" in sacrifice (Moses 5:5). To sacrifice an animal. I wonder what Adam and Eve thought when they received this commandment. They had come from a place of no death and no pain and no blood, and now they were being asked to kill one of their lambs. I once saw an exhibit in a wax museum that depicted this bloody scene. Adam had an emotionally wrecked face, and Eve was turned away with a look of being nauseated. I cannot imagine the torment of soul as they watched the life drain out of their little fluffy. A HEARTBREAKING MOMENT.

"After many days, an angel of the Lord appeared unto Adam, saying: Why dost thou offer sacrifices unto the Lord?" Adam, why are you doing this? "And Adam said unto him: I KNOW NOT, SAVE THE LORD COMMANDED ME" (Moses 5:6). I have no idea. I'm only doing it because God asked me to. Bless his obedient heart! And then the angel gave him an explanation.

"THIS THING IS A SIMILITUDE OF THE SACRIFICE OF THE ONLY BEGOTTEN OF THE FATHER, WHICH IS FULL OF GRACE AND TRUTH" (MOSES 5:7).

He told Adam and Eve, essentially, that this was the answer to their question about how to get back into the presence of God. It would be through a heartbreaking, nauseating, SACRIFICIAL DEATH OF AN INNOCENT CREATURE—

the Savior, Jesus—the Lamb.

Let's fast-forward time a little bit to chapter two in the Story of the Lamb—the tale of Abraham and Isaac. Do you remember this story? It's in Genesis 22. Abraham and Sarah waited their whole lives to have a baby. Perhaps they had already given up on that dream when God sent messengers to tell Sarah the good news: she would have a little boy. She giggled in response—perhaps in surprise or a little bit of disbelief. But then that little boy came, and they named him Isaac—their miracle son!

Then one day, the Lord came to Abraham with a terrible request: "Take now thy son, thine only son Isaac, whom thou lovest, . . . and offer him there for a burnt offering upon one of the mountains which I will tell thee of" (Genesis 22:2). How could Abraham do such a thing? His precious son! The mountain that God sent Abraham and Isaac to was a three-day journey away. I imagine that Abraham didn't sleep a wink during that trip, and each step closer to their destination brought a mountain of hurt to his heart.

As they arrived at the place, Isaac pointed out to his father that they had stones, sticks, and fire, but "WHERE iS THE LAMB FOR A BURNT OffERING?" (v. 7).

Abraham responded back,

"My son, God will provide himself a lamb" (v. 8).

You probably know the end of the story. Isaac was tied up on the altar, and just as Abraham was about to fulfill the commandment to sacrifice his son, an angel appeared to stop him. They were spared! I love that part! And then the two of them looked over and noticed "a ram caught in a thicket by his horns" (v. 13). The ram was then offered up in the place of Isaac on the altar.

WHAT CAN WE MAKE FROM THIS STORY?

Think about these details we get from the book of Genesis:

A LOVING FATHER WITH A MIRACLE CHILD.

A THREE-DAY JOURNEY.

WOOD CARRIED UP THE HILL BY THE BOY ON HIS BACK.

A STORY OF SACRIFICE OF A BELOVED SON.

Whose story does that sound like to you?

For a while I wondered why God sent them to a far-away mountain for this sacrifice. Why not one behind their house? Perhaps it is because of where that mountain range is. Years later, that very mountain range that Abraham and Isaac went to would have places called Golgotha and Calvary (see 2 Chronicles 3:1). It was the same mountain range where Jesus was sacrificed and died. In Abraham's day, a ram was found to replace his son. But do you remember what animal Abraham said God would provide?

A LAMB.

GOD WAS STILL GOING TO PROVIDE A LAMB IN THAT SAME SPOT, BUT IT WOULDN'T HAPPEN FOR ANOTHER TWO THOUSAND YEARS.

It was a LAMB that would TAKE THE PLACE OF ALL OF US on that altar. Abraham named the mountain place as they left "Jehovah-jireh," which means, "In the mount of the Lord it shall be seen"

(Genesis 22:14). A mount where a sacrificing Father laid His Son, the Lamb, on an altar.

Let's fast-forward a little more time to another little chapter in this Story of the Lamb. Now we go to Egypt, where the children of Israel had been slaves for several hundred years. THEY HAD PRAYED AND CRIED FOR DELIVERANCE, and the Lord sent Moses to lead them out. Unfortunately, Pharaoh was stubborn and prideful and would not let them go, so the Lord sent plagues into Egypt to try to humble him. For nine plagues, the Pharaoh waffled back and forth. A plague would come and Pharaoh would promise to let them go if the plague went away. Once the plague went away, he would change his mind. This happened through the frogs and the lice and the flies and the disease and the rivers turning to blood. Finally, the Lord warned them of a plague that would be worse than all the rest. On a given night, a destruction was going to pass through all of Egypt at midnight and "all the firstborn in the land of Egypt shall die, from the firstborn of Pharoah . . . even unto the firstborn of the maidservant" (Exodus 11:4–5).

This plague would be the hardest of all. Give me all the frogs and lice in the world—but please do not take my oldest child. Everyone would have to face this plague—no matter who they were. In the previous plagues, the children of Israel were spared, but this one could impact all of them. However, after announcing the plague, the Lord gave Moses instructions in HOW TO BE SAVED from it.

Anyone who wanted to be spared from the destroying angel needed to get a

"lamb without blemish"

who was a firstborn male (Exodus 12:5). "Without blemish" means without any spots or imperfections. The lamb came into their houses on the tenth day of the month and would stay until the fourteenth day. On the fourteenth day, at sunset, they were to kill the lamb, roast it, and eat it with unleavened bread and other food items. Then they were to take the blood from the lamb and wipe it on the doorposts of their house. Any house that was marked by the blood of the lamb would be passed over on the dreaded night. And so it happened. Families gathered firstborn male lambs without any spots or blemishes and brought them into their homes on the tenth day. For three days they probably fell in love with their lamb, got to know its personality, and some may have even named it. Then on the last night, they killed the beloved little lamb and put its blood on their doorposts. Anyone who was the oldest child would probably have been particularly emotional that night. As they sat for dinner, they would have looked at the lamb on the table and perhaps thought,

"The only reason I am going to live is because that lamb died in my place."

This is a tradition that the Lord asked them to continue to do year after year. It has become what you and I might know as the Passover (we will talk about this again in a minute). It is an event He wanted them to always remember—the night He saved them from the plague and delivered them from Egypt. There are some plagues, like that final one, that will affect all of us. One of those is justice and the effects of the Fall. No matter who we are, or how many service projects we have gone to, or the number of baptisms for the dead we have performed, or punk kids we've been nice to, if we tried to face sin and death on our own, we would be toast.

BUT THOSE OF US WHO ARE COVERED

BY THE BLOOD OF THE LAMB WILL BE PASSED OVER.

The effects of sin and death will not be permanent for us. The children of Israel were saved that night because

A LAMB DIED IN THEIR PLACE.

That can be the thesis statement of our story too.

All throughout the history of the Old Testament, the people were commanded to offer up sacrifices in the name of the Lord. Once Moses built his portable temple, and then when King Solomon built a permanent one, most of these were offered on an altar in these holy places. One of the offerings that was made was called a sin offering. This was done as a part of repentance for sins against God. The Lord outlined in the book of Leviticus how these were to be done (see Leviticus 1:1–9). A person would bring their lamb (a male without blemish) to the door of the temple, where a temple priest would meet them. Once there, the person making the offering—the person repenting of sin—would place his or her hands on the head of the lamb as a symbolic way of transferring sin to the lamb. The priest would then hand the person a knife to kill the lamb as a symbolic substitution punishment for the sins. I heard a teacher once talk about a time in seminary when a class was going through this lesson. As the teacher explained the sin offering, everyone listened silently. But when he tried to move on, a girl raised her hand in protest. "THEY DID WHAT?!" she asked. "THAT IS NOT RIGHT!" she yelled out. For the next while, members of the class tried to convince her that it was okay. They used arguments like, "Don't worry, they would eat part of it afterwards." Or, "It was part of life back then." Or, "They did it all the time." No matter what argument they offered, the girl fought back. She refused to accept it as okay. The teacher let the arguing go on. And then the girl said this:

"NO, NO. YOU AREN'T UNDERSTANDING. THIS ISN'T FAIR. IT IS NOT RIGHT THAT THE LAMB SHOULD DIE FOR SOMETHING THE PERSON DID WRONG."

The teacher then said, "She is the only one in the room who actually gets it. IT IS NOT FAIR THAT AN INNOCENT CREATURE SHOULD DIE FOR THE SINS THAT I HAVE COMMITTED." And isn't that true? Jesus should not have to suffer for something I have done wrong. It really isn't fair. That is why it is called

mercy and love.

Let's go to one more chapter in this Book of the Lamb—this one in the New Testament. It is a story that can be found at the end of each of the Gospels. Jesus was with His disciples in an upper room somewhere in Jerusalem. They were gathered at the time of Passover. Remember that for hundreds of years, faithful Saints gathered as families and friends to reenact and remember the night God saved them all from the plague and from Egypt. They would talk about the food on the table and its symbolism for the night of the rescue. They ate UNLEAVENED BREAD as a remembrance of how quickly they had to leave (unleavened bread is bread that hasn't had time to rise—it is made quickly). They ate BITTER HERBS because of the bitterness of slavery, and they drank WINE to symbolize the celebration of the redemption from slavery to the Egyptians.

On this night, however, Jesus introduced a new script with new symbols. Instead of talking about the items on the table in reference to the miracle of Egypt, He taught them a new story. As He picked up the bread, He broke and tore it and told the disciples to eat it in remembrance of His body—a body that would be broken and torn for them. As they drank the wine, they drank it in remembrance of His blood, which He would shed for them (see Matthew 26:17–30).

> ## On that night, Jesus changed the ordinance from sacrifice to sacrament.

Interestingly, none of the Gospel writers mention the most important element on the table. They mention the bread and the wine, but not the lamb—the main course! That might be because the LAMB OF GOD WAS NOT ON THE TABLE, BUT SITTING AT THE TABLE. After that very meal, Jesus went into Gethsemane and then onto Calvary's cross the next day to become the Passover Lamb. THE LAMB THAT WOULD SAVE THEM ALL FROM DEATH.

Each week as we gather for the holy sacrament, we remember these same stories. Priests stand behind an altar, and on that sacred table are bread and water that represent the death and sacrifice of Jesus Christ, the Lamb.

It is no wonder that John chose to call Jesus by that name. With a simple phrase—

"BEHOLD THE LAMB OF GOD"

—John could remind everyone there of who He was. "There He is," he could have said. "That is ADAM AND EVE'S LAMB that would take them back to the presence of God. There is ISAAC'S LAMB—the one who would die in His place. There is the TEMPLE LAMB who will suffer our penalty of sin. The PASSOVER LAMB who will spill His blood to save us from death." It's no wonder He was born right near shepherd fields. In those days, shepherds would be out at night waiting for baby lambs to be born—lambs that would be used on the temple altars. They would need to check all the firstborn males for blemishes—and if they found one without spot, that lamb was wrapped up and laid on the stable floor, set aside for sacrifice. And that first night of Christmas, a baby was born, and laid in a stable, wrapped up in swaddling clothes, set aside for sacrifice—the Lamb of God—an unexpected hero. One that was MIGHTY AND POWERFUL ENOUGH TO BEAT THE DRAGON but who would do it BY HUMBLY, MEEKLY, AND INNOCENTLY LYING DOWN ON THE ALTAR. He won everything by giving everything. And by so doing, He became our everything.

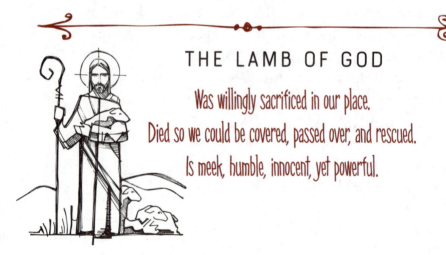

THE LAMB OF GOD

Was willingly sacrificed in our place.
Died so we could be covered, passed over, and rescued.
Is meek, humble, innocent, yet powerful.

9

THE LOYAL ADVOCATE

I love people. All humans of all kinds. The second great commandment—to love people—is one of my favorites. Whenever I pass crowds on the street or people-watch at a mall, they fascinate and intrigue me. I want to know their stories. Where are they from? Why are they here? What is their favorite pair of shoes? Whenever I get the chance, I like meeting people while waiting in lines, riding in Ubers, or talking story with the person next to me on the airplane. I am not that guy who puts in headphones right when I sit down in my airplane seat (although if our conversation doesn't start before takeoff, I am out like a light).

I meet new friends and talk life. I once heard the whole life story of my new friend Brother Bob on my flight to Maui. He told me all about his shenanigans in high school, his adventures at war, and his deep spiritual, miraculous experiences lying in a hospital bed. "I've never told anyone this story," he said to me when our flight was over. I am so glad he did. I cried together with another new friend named Jeff, the New Mexico cowboy, on the way to his brother's funeral in Arizona. We had a big hug when we got off the plane. Haven't seen him since. I also have listened to a full half hour of nonstop emotional fast talking from Victoria on my way to Texas—all in Portuguese. I don't speak a lick of Portuguese, but I pretended I did because I felt like she wanted someone to listen to her. This kind of stuff thrills my soul.

I once asked someone I didn't know very well a kind of personal question—not ultra personal, just minor league level—and she responded by asking me, "What is my favorite ice cream flavor?" I was confused. She asked again, "Do you know my favorite ice cream flavor?"

I guessed. "Strawberry."

"Nope."

Pity. Then she said, "If you don't know my favorite ice cream flavor, then we aren't close enough for you to ask that question."

Of course, my next question to her was, "So, what's your favorite ice cream flavor?"

"Nice try," is all I got back.

We all have different levels of relationships with people. Even though I like all people and call them friends, I don't open up and share things with all of them the same way. There are some I trust more, some I like more, and some I understand more. And I am committed more to some than others. This is true of all of us, right? If someone asked me for a favor, I would be more or less willing to do it depending on how close we were as friends and how big of a favor it was. What level of friend would I go pick up from the airport? And who would I pick up at three in the morning? Who would I give my last popsicle to? Who would I get a papercut for? These all depend on the kind of friend the person is.

When I asked my friend Landon (who loves cookies and cream, by the way) what his favorite name for Jesus was in the scriptures, he quickly replied,

"ADVOCATE."

I was writing this book and didn't have that as one of the names I had chosen, so I wanted to know why. I wanted him to win me over to it. He said, "I started to love that one several years ago in high school. I think it struck a chord in me because I didn't feel like I had any other advocate in my life. Yeah, I had lots of friends, but no one who I felt truly had my back.

Someone who knew me and loved me. Who would catch me when I fell. Who would plead for me. Who would argue my case.

Who would never forget me. So when I learned that Christ was our Advocate—a friend like that—I loved it!" Right when he said it, I adored the definition for Advocate he was giving to me. It was a description of the Jesus I find in scripture. SOMEONE WHO TRULY HAS YOUR BACK, someone who would plead for you, and someone who would never forget you. Someone you could trust with everything. All because He knows and loves you.

To some of the first missionaries in this dispensation, the Lord said,

"LIFT UP YOUR HEARTS AND BE GLAD, FOR I AM IN YOUR MIDST, AND AM YOUR ADVOCATE" (D&C 29:5).

I love how He cheers them up by reminding them that He would be one of their companions. Some of their other companions could have been some doozies. The name Advocate comes from a Latin word that means someone who is a voice for you or someone who pleads for another.[15] The word can also be translated as an intercessor, helper, or comforter.[16]

To advocate means to fight or defend a cause.

That would be a fantastic companion! How does Jesus live and love like an advocate?

Not long before He entered into the Garden of Gethsemane, the Lord prayed to the Father in a prayer that has been called the Great Intercessory Prayer. The word *intercessor* is another synonym for advocate. It is a title that describes someone who is willing to intervene or intercede on someone else's behalf. Someone willing to step into a situation to help. You can read the whole stunning prayer in John chapter 17, but here is just a sneak peek of it for you. "I PRAY FOR THEM . . . FOR THEY ARE THINE. . . . I pray not that thou shouldest take them out of the world, but that thou shouldest keep them from the evil. . . . Sanctify them through thy truth: thy word is truth" (John 17:9, 15–17). Don't you love the image of Jesus kneeling, pleading, and praying for you? That is part of what it means to be an advocate—to plead for someone else. In this case, that someone else is you, and that Advocate is Jesus.

One of the reasons Jesus makes a ☆ perfect Advocate is because ☆ He knows us so well.

Perfectly, in fact. He knows our weaknesses, our temptations, and our trials. He knows exactly how each of us feels in every situation. WE NEVER CAN SAY THAT WE ARE COMPLETELY ALONE OR THAT NO ONE UNDERSTANDS US, BECAUSE SOMEONE ALWAYS DOES. The great missionary prophet Alma once taught about Jesus that "he will take upon him their infirmities, that his bowels may be filled with mercy, according to the flesh, that he may know according to the flesh how to succor his people according to their infirmities" (Alma 7:12). Infirmities are the stuff of life. The sicknesses, the sorrows, the sadnesses. Jesus knows according to the flesh what we experience and feel. THAT MEANS HE DOESN'T JUST HAVE SYMPATHY FOR US; HE HAS EMPATHY. HE KNOWS IT. And because He knows it, Alma says He can succor us, His people. *Succor* is a word that means "run to."

> HE RUNS TO US IN OUR TIMES OF NEED
> BECAUSE HE KNOWS EXACTLY WHAT IS
> WRONG AND PRECISELY HOW TO HANDLE IT.
> HE IS NEVER AT A LOSS FOR THE RIGHT
> THING TO SAY OR THE RIGHT THING TO DO IN
> ANY GIVEN SITUATION. HE NEVER MOSEYS
> OR HANGS BACK. HE RUNS RIGHT IN.

I think about this every time I read the parable of the prodigal son. Do you remember that one? The one where the younger brother takes his inheritance and leaves the father's farm to go off and live a wild and riotous life. When he wasted it all and was down, dirty, and depressed in a pigsty, he decided to go back home. He was met by his merciful and forgiving father, who ran to him, scooped him up in a papa-bear squeeze, and said, "For this my son was dead, and is alive again; HE WAS LOST, AND IS FOUND" (Luke 15:24). That is easily my all-time favorite scene in the whole Bible. Just saying.

Once while reading this parable, I was struck in my heart by the phrase "LOST AND FOUND." Just so you know, I am the king of losing things—keys, wallets, shoes, everything!—so I might be particularly sensitive to it. This parable of the prodigal son comes as the last parable Jesus shared in a set of three. The first one is about a lost lamb, the second a lost coin (the one we already talked about), and this one—a lost boy. In the first two parables, WHEN THE LAMB AND COIN ARE LOST, SOMEONE GOES OUT into the wilderness or lights candles and goes through the whole house LOOKING FOR THE THINGS THAT WERE LOST. Under the couch cushions, in the junk drawer, behind the tree, down the cliff, under the bed. Everywhere! And when the object is found, they throw a party!

In this last parable, though, THERE IS SOMETHING DIFFERENT. No one goes out looking for the boy when he didn't come home. No one runs in! And to make it even more shocking, the story tells us he has an older brother. Now look, the older brother's reaction in the parable of the prodigal son makes sense. Of course he didn't go looking for the younger brother. He wasted the family money. He ran off like a punk. He didn't deserve to be rescued or loved. He didn't deserve to be found and celebrated. It was all his fault. Those sound like lines or thoughts the older brother could have had. But I am an older brother, and that part stings me every time. Older brothers should go out looking for lost siblings. It is what they do.

I read a story not too long ago about two brothers who were stationed together on the *USS Arizona* at Pearl Harbor during the infamous attack. When the ship was bombed on an early Sunday morning, John, the older brother of the two, was dragged out, injured and dazed, and put onto a rescue boat of wounded soldiers that took off back to the shore for safety. As the lifeboat pulled away from the sinking battleship, John realized what was going on and immediately started looking around the life raft for his younger brother. When he didn't see him, he yelled, "I can't go; my brother's back in there!" Their rescue raft was too far from the wreckage, and no one was turning back. But the second it got to shore, he pushed his way through the crowds, jumped into another little boat, and went back onto the sinking and smoking ship looking for his brother. NO AMOUNT OF DANGER OR FIRE OR WARNINGS COULD STOP HIM. HE WAS GOING TO FIND HIS LOST BROTHER.[17] He went running in.

Every time I read the parable of the prodigal son and I get to the part where no one goes looking for him, it leaves me wishing for an older brother like John to be in the story. Someone to push through a crowd, abandon reason, and recklessly run into the fire looking for his little brother. I want to add a scene to the parable. One where the father sobs at the dinner table and tells the rest of the family that his son is gone and lost. I want him to call out between cries with his face buried in his hands: "Who will find my boy? Who will bring him home?" And then I want the older brother to stand up and say this line: "Send me, father. I'll go." SOMETIMES I WONDER IF JESUS LEFT THAT PART OUT OF THE STORY SO THAT WE WOULD WISH FOR A BROTHER LIKE THAT.

A million years ago, before we were born, our Heavenly Parents were on the edge of sending Their cherished children into this warzone world when They gathered us together. The Father of us all knew we would be lost and sinking some days and would need someone to come looking for us. He asked for a volunteer. A Rescuer. An Advocate. One who would and could run into the fire in rescue. "WHOM SHALL I SEND?" the Father asked. And out of the crowd, Jesus—the older brother the story needed—raised His hand up and replied,

(Abraham 3:27).

I'll go. Just like the scene I want to add to the parable. Except this one was in real life.

That kind of loyalty and love bookends our whole story. Jesus stood by us before the world was created and will still be standing there by us in the closing-up scenes, too. I don't know what the Final Judgment day will look like, but sometimes I imagine it as a courtroom. I see myself standing there alone, worried about the overloaded evidence table and the line of witnesses to speak out against me. Then I imagine the judge asking, "Is there anyone here willing to claim this boy? Is there anyone here willing to speak for him? Who is willing to defend and advocate the case of a clearly guilty criminal? The evidence against him is stacked!"

Then I imagine hearing a response like this one: "Listen to him who is the **ADVOCATE WITH THE FATHER, WHO IS PLEADING YOUR CAUSE BEFORE HIM**—Saying: Father, behold the sufferings and death of him who did no sin, in whom thou wast well pleased; behold the blood of thy Son which was shed, the blood of him whom thou gavest that thyself might be glorified;

> Wherefore, Father, spare these my brethren that believe on my name, that they may come unto me and have everlasting life" (D&C 45:3–5).

An advocate in a court of law is someone who chooses to defend you. Typically, lawyers aren't willing to defend cases they know they cannot win, and especially cases where the accused is clearly guilty. But Jesus has never been typical. He chooses to stand by and defend us knowing full well what we have done. Did you see that line in the scripture we just looked at? What He says as our Advocate? "Behold the sufferings and death of him who did no sin." **LOOK AT ME,** He seems to say. **NOT AT THE GUILTY ONE.** What Jesus has done will have an infinitely greater impact on our futures than what we have done. He came and lived out a perfect life for us. The life we should have lived. He also came and defeated sin and death and the grasp that Satan has on us. And He did this even knowing everything that He knows. We might think to ourselves, oh, if He knew what kind of person I actually am, He would not stick around. If He knew the things I have done, He would never stand in my place. The beautiful truth is—He does. He knows everything and was still willing to go to the cross for us. He fought for us. For a cause He believed in.

HE WAS AND IS OUR CHAMPION.

During a great battle in the Bible, the Israelites and Philistines were in a final showdown fight in the valley called Elah. The kind of final battle scene you find in the best movies. If the Philistines could make it through this particular valley, they would have access to the center of Israel. The whole kingdom would fall into their hands. Everything hung in the balance. It all came down to this. This is a battle you can read about in 1 Samuel 17. One of the rules of war in those ancient times was that EACH ARMY COULD CHOOSE A CHAMPION TO FIGHT FOR AND IN BEHALF OF THE REST OF THE ARMY. Instead of wasting so much life and resources, the two competing armies would choose a single person for one-on-one combat that determined the entire battle. The side that lost would have to surrender their entire army as slaves to the side that won. The Philistines chose a giant named Goliath as their champion. He was a brute! Tall and strong and mighty! He was around nine feet tall (which means he could dunk without jumping or standing on tiptoes) and covered with armor. He held a spear that weighed over a hundred pounds and a shield so big he had another warrior carry it for him (see 1 Samuel 17:4–7). I would hate that job! GOLIATH HAD BEEN TRAINED AS A WARRIOR SINCE HE WAS A YOUNG BOY and was an easy pick for the Philistine army. For forty days, the Israelites were shaking in their boots and hiding in the mountainside camp, unable to decide on a soldier to send out. This was a fight that would end in certain death. They desperately needed someone, anyone, willing and able to fight for them. But who volunteers to be slaughtered? For forty days Goliath taunted the children of Israel. Like a bully.

And then came DAViD, A SHEPHERD BoY WHo WAS Too YoUNG To BE A SoLDiER. He was sent by his father from his hometown of Bethlehem with a package of breads and cheeses for his older brothers on the front line (for some reason I love that he came with cheese). When he got to the battlefield, he saw and heard Goliath shouting out swears and insults against the army of the Lord. He couldn't believe his ears. As he asked more about it, his older brother got after him for staying in the battle and making a scene. Just leave, David! David responded in one of my favorite verses of scripture: "What have I now done? Is there not a cause?" (1 Samuel 17:29). Isn't there a cause worth fighting for here? Are we not defending our family, our country, our friends, and our God? David then went to the king and said,

"Let no man's heart fail because of him; thy servant will go and fight" (v. 32).

I will go, he said. He would defend the army. HE WoULD Go iN THEiR PLACE. An intercessor warrior. And that is exactly what he did.

Little David went into the battlefield against Goliath with only a sling and five stones from a nearby river. The Philistines laughed and the Israelites held their breath. Everything was on the line. I wonder how David felt when he walked into the valley, on the front

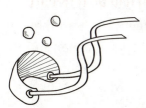

lines, alone. Was he scared? Did he feel the pressure of the seriousness of the fight? We aren't sure what was happening in his heart, but the scriptures say what he said and did: "I come to thee in the name of the Lord of hosts, the God of the armies of Israel. . . . THiS DAY WiLL THE LORD DELiVER THEE iNTO MiNE HAND" (1 Samuel 17:45–46). David then ran toward Goliath with reckless abandon and a sling, and he brought down the giant. He won. He won for Israel. He had fought their battle and defeated their enemy for them. And then David took the sword of Goliath and cut off the giant's head. The army of Israel shouted for joy!

Every time I read this story, I think about another champion. Our champion, Jesus. When we hear the taunts of our enemies—sin and death and weakness—saying,

"You'll never be enough!

WE HAVE YOU DEFEATED!

YOUR SIN!

Your addiction!

IT IS TOO MUCH FOR YOU!

We claim you now!"

We may shake in our boots. Maybe they are right. Maybe we have lost. This is a battle we cannot win. I'm not strong enough. I'm not brave enough. And then the man from Bethlehem came, sent by His Father, into the front lines of the battle. Was He scared? Did He know the pressure that was on Him? Everything was on the line. Knowing the risks and the cost, He still came running in. From the very beginning He has been choosing to fight for and in behalf of us—to stand in our place—with His simple yet brave response to the Father: "Here am I, send me" (Abraham 3:27). That wasn't all talk.

He came and He fought and He won. And He cut off the head of our enemy to no more rise again. Our sin has no power to live once He comes into the battle. Once our Advocate speaks, all enemies will be silent. They have no more claim.

He thought there was a cause worth fighting for. That cause was us.

In the book of Hebrews, the writer pleads for people to look "unto Jesus the author and finisher of our faith; who for the joy that was set before him endured the cross" (Hebrews 12:2). I love the line, "the joy that was set before Him." THAT iS you. THAT iS ME. THAT iS HOW HE ENDURED THE CROSS—THROUGH THE JOY THAT you ARE TO HiM. It was worth it. You were worth it.

You cannot find another friend like Jesus in all the universe. One who knows everything and still is willing to give everything in defense of you. Joseph Smith once said, "I would esteem it one of the greatest blessings, if I am to be afflicted in this world, to have my lot cast where I can find brothers and friends all around me."[18] One of Joseph's fiercely faithful friends was a man named Willard Richards. "The Doctor," as Joseph affectionately called him, went with Joseph into Carthage Jail on the day he was martyred. He had not been arrested and he was not forced to go, but he went because he wanted to stand by Joseph to the end. On the day of the martyrdom, as the army approached, Joseph asked Willard if he would be willing to go into the cell with them. He answered, "'Brother Joseph, you did not ask me to cross the river with you—you did not ask me to come to Carthage—you did not ask me to come to jail with you— and do you think I would forsake you now? But I will tell you what I will do; if you are condemned to be hung for treason, I will be hung in your stead, and you shall go free.' Joseph said, 'You cannot.' [He] replied, 'I will.'"[19]

That story sends chills down my spine every time. There is a lot of Jesus in that friendship. I WISH AND HOPE THAT LIKE JOSEPH, YOU ARE SURROUNDED BY DEAR FRIENDS YOUR WHOLE LIFE. I hope you have defenders, champions, a tribe, a posse, your homies, your girls, your people to stand by you for all your days. I hope you cross through the veil of death and are greeted by a dogpile of old chums. I hope you have friends who will pick you up from the airport at three in the morning and give you their last popsicle. Many of you certainly have at least one other someone who loves and adores and cares about you more wildly than they should—for most of you, that's your mom.

> But no matter who you have in your contact lists, who you hang out with every Friday night, what your experiences are in this life, or what battles you are called to fight, you should know that you have a loyal, faithful friend and advocate in Jesus.

You don't have that type of guarantee with anyone else in your life. One day, a friend of mine told me a story about his neighbors, who were all piling into their minivan to head off to Grandma's house. (Yes, I have friends with minivans. You will too someday.) Their youngest was a little baby who was still in a car seat. When the dad went to buckle in some of the other kids, he set the car seat on top of the van so that he could use both hands to wrestle the other hoodlums in. The dad finished his buckle duties and the mom finished hers, and then they both climbed into their front seats, forgetting about the baby! They pulled out of their driveway, and right as they slowed at the stop sign that was by their corner house, the mom looked over in horror at her husband and yelled, "The baby!!" He jumped out of the minivan and looked on top of the roof to find the car seat still rocking back and forth from the stop of the car, with the baby happily giggling in-side. He pulled down the baby, opened the side door, clicked the seat in, got back in his seat, and the two of them drove in shocked silence all the way to their destination.

That story still gets me every time! It will take a solid ten min-utes for my heart rate to go back down. But it also reminds me of a scripture from Isaiah: "Can a woman forget her [nursing] child, that she should not have compassion on the son of her womb?" Is it pos-sible for a mom to forget her newborn baby? "Yea, THEY MAY FORGET," Isaiah says—it is possible. Even a mom and a dad can forget their little babies. "YET WILL I NOT FORGET THEE. BEHOLD, I HAVE GRAVEN THEE UPON THE PALMS OF MY HANDS" (Isaiah 49:15–16). But He doesn't. You are in His hands as a permanent reminder.

> MOMS, DADS, RELATIVES, NEIGHBORS, AND LIFELONG FRIENDS MIGHT FAIL YOU, BUT HE WON'T.

If you fall, He will catch you every time. You will always have someone who has your back. Someone who will defend your case. Someone who will plead for you. Someone who won't forget about you. Your name will always be safe with Him. He will never gossip or talk behind your back. All His words about you will always be kind. He will never betray you or abandon you or do anything that would hurt you. He knows everything about you—your trials, your temptations, your struggles, your worries, and your sins. **YOU CAN PUT ALL OF YOUR TRUST IN HIM. HE IS EVER FAITHFUL. HE IS FOR YOU.** You have an Advocate who speaks for, pleads for, stands up for, fights for, and goes out looking for you. "There I will be also," He said. "For I will go before your face. I will be on your right hand and on your left, and my Spirit shall be in your hearts, and mine angels round about you, to bear you up" (D&C 84:88). With Jesus, each of us can have Joseph's wish and always be surrounded by defenders and friends. And like Willard Richards, **JESUS WASN'T ONLY WILLING TO BE HUNG IN OUR PLACE, BUT HE WAS HUNG IN OUR PLACE ON CALVARY'S CROSS.** He did **COME RUNNING** into the fire for you. He did volunteer to take your place. He will **DEFEND YOU** all the way to the end. No one ever has to walk into the courtroom or into the valley alone. He will **TAKE YOUR SIDE** and be on your side every time. And He definitely knows your favorite flavor of ice cream.

THE LOYAL ADVOCATE

Will defend you, fight for you, and stand by you.

Pleads to the Father for you and your cause.

Will never abandon or forget you.

10

THE ANTICIPATED KING

Have you ever heard the story, whether it is true or not, about the class with the surprise paper assignment for their final grade? Sorry if this stresses you out. I shouldn't make you think about school. But it goes like this: On the first day of class, the professor explained to the students that their grade for the course would be based on one paper they would turn in. No tests, no quizzes, and no other assignments. Just this one paper. The details for it were explained on a worksheet that she handed out, but it purposely had one bit of iMPORTANT iNFORMATiON MiSSiNG. THE DUE DATE. And that was the catch. The day was set for when the paper was due, but only the teacher knew when that was. It was a surprise. She explained that they would have plenty of time to finish it, but one day when they got there, she would call for those papers. If the students were in class and they had done their assignment, they would get a grade. If they weren't, and they hadn't, then they wouldn't. One paper. One unknown due date. All or nothing.

The first time I heard this story it was in church. It was supposed to be an analogy for the Second Coming of Jesus. There is a day set when He will return. He knows when it is.

We have plenty of time to prepare, but we don't know when it will actually be.

One day, we will just wake up and He will be here. Ready or not.

I guess the analogy is sort of okay, but it also gives me anxiety. I wouldn't look forward to the day at all. Yes, it makes me want to prepare, but it does not give me something to look forward to. It is preparation out of fear. It makes me nervous and lose sleep. I have another analogy for the Second Coming I like a thousand times better.

What if Christmas weren't on a set date? What if you got an announcement from the North Pole that Christmas was coming, but it would not be on the 25th? The date was going to be a surprise. Sometime in the month of December everyone would just wake up and it would be Christmas morning. The lights on the tree would be on and there would be presents and good food and music and candy and everything else you look forward to on Christmas morning. Thinking about that makes me so excited. CAN YOU iMAGiNE WHAT THAT MONTH WOULD BE LiKE?? Everyone knows Christmas is close—we were told it was. But we don't know when exactly. That means we all go to bed every night bubbling with anticipation. It could be in the morning! We could just wake up and it will be Christmas!! Our eyes would pop open and our first whisper would be, "Maybe today!" We would run down the stairs and peek around the corner to see if it had come. Don't you love that idea? I'm sending a request up north. That, my friends, is a better analogy for the Second Coming. Not an assignment due, but Christmas morning!

I HOPE YOU AREN'T SCARED OF THE SECOND COMING.

If anyone has ever taught you about the Second Coming and made you feel fear, that person taught it wrong.

There are some scary things associated with the Second Coming (earthquakes and diseases with no cure and blood moons), but Jesus is not one of those scary things.

Jesus is coming back. The one who healed the sick, was tender to the woman caught in sin, and raised the dead. That Jesus. The Jesus that we have read about, sung about, and wished for is the Jesus who will actually arrive. The one who took on death and sin as a champion for us all. Him!

AND WHEN HE COMES, HE WILL RIDE IN WITH TRIUMPHANT GLORY ON HIS WHITE HORSE AS KING OF KINGS

(see Revelation 19:16).

THIS IS ONE OF HIS NAMES.

In ancient times, so much depended on the king. The prosperity of the nation and the people was based on the way he ran the economy. The king was in charge of protecting the people and defending them against threats. He was responsible for creating laws that were fair and for upholding them at all times. The king made sure everything was all right in the kingdom. All things were under his direction and control.

Today, fear and bullies and sin and chaos seem to rule the world. The laws that people live by are more like the laws of the jungle—a dog-eat-dog world. But when He comes again, Isaiah said,

"THE WOLF ALSO SHALL DWELL WITH THE LAMB, AND THE LEOPARD SHALL LIE DOWN WITH THE KID. . . . THEY SHALL NOT HURT NOR DESTROY IN ALL MY HOLY MOUNTAIN: FOR THE EARTH SHALL BE FULL OF THE KNOWLEDGE OF THE LORD, AS THE WATERS COVER THE SEA" (ISAIAH 11:6, 9).

He will lead with attributes of mercy, justice, hope, and grace. His LAWS OF LOVE will protect and uphold His people in a way that lets them thrive. Isaiah also said, "The government shall be upon his shoulder: and his name shall be called Wonderful, Counsellor, The mighty God, The everlasting Father, The PRINCE OF PEACE. Of the increase of his government and peace there shall be no end" (Isaiah 9:6–7).

He will reign in wonderful ways, gentle ways, mighty ways, and peaceful ways.

And they will last forever and ever. Under His care, all of the unfair things of this world will be made right. The losses that people had will be made up to them. The burdens that people carried will be replaced with blessings untold. I look forward to that day like nothing else I can think of. I am not sure when it will happen, and I don't know how it will happen, but I do know that one day in the future, Jesus will be coming back to this world, and that makes my heart want to explode with the excitement of a thousand fireworks. That is supposed to be the most anticipated day ever. THE CHRISTMAS MORNING OF ALL CHRISTMAS MORNINGS.

The first Christmas morning, Jesus came to a meek and humble manger. Most of His life was lived without fanciness or fanfare. There was one occasion, though, when we got a glimpse of Him as a king. The week of His death, Jesus rode into Jerusalem in an event we call the Triumphal Entry. And while He rode in, the people lined the streets as if they were watching a ROYAL PARADE. "And a very great multitude spread their garments in the way; others cut down branches from the trees, and strawed them in the way. And

the multitudes that went before, and that followed, cried, saying, Hosanna to the Son of David: Blessed is he that cometh in the name of the Lord; Hosanna in the highest" (Matthew 21:8–9). The people cheered and WAVED THEIR PALM BRANCHES and shouted Hosanna as He rode in. It was almost as if they were participating in a dress rehearsal of what the whole world will do when He returns.

John saw a vision of the Savior's Second Coming and said, "I heard as it were the voice of a great multitude, and as the voice of many waters, and as the voice of mighty thunderings, saying, Alleluia: for the Lord God omnipotent reigneth. Let us be glad and rejoice, and give honour to him: for the marriage of the Lamb is come" (Revelation 19:6–7).

Don't you love that His Second Coming is described as a wedding feast? A celebration! Weddings have good music and cake and cheers and chocolate fountains.

His return will be a day of praise and a day of presents.

Did you know that Jesus's first recorded miracle in the New Testament happened at a wedding? It was His miracle of turning water to wine. It seems like such a funny miracle to perform as His first one. This would be His leadoff miracle. His first one! His introduction. I don't know about you, but I would pick something much cooler. Why not raise a whole city from the dead or something? I feel like He would want to teach everyone who He really was through this first miracle. BUT MAYBE HE DID.

Running out of wine at a wedding in Jesus's day was a big deal. You don't ever run out of refreshments at a wedding. It's a big no-no. Super embarrassing for the bride and groom. Mary, Jesus's mom, who seemed to have some job at the wedding, came to Him for help. We have run out of wine, she said. He directed some of the workers to grab six waterpots that were used for purification in the temple. They quite possibly could have been the water containers used to wash hands and feet before participating in temple ordinances. The gross water. Feet water. Each of those pots held about twenty to thirty gallons. The servants filled them to the brim with water, and then Jesus turned the water into wedding wine. When the wine was taken to the governor of the feast, he was shocked. Usually, people set out the best wine at the beginning of a wedding to make an impression on those who were there. Once the night wore on and people were tired and drunk and wouldn't notice, the cheap, off-brand wine was brought out. But surprisingly, as the governor said, "THOU HAST KEPT THE GOOD WINE UNTIL NOW" (John 2:10). YOU SAVED THE BEST FOR LAST.

What seems to be a miracle that keeps a bride and groom from being embarrassed at their wedding party might actually be teaching us a little bit more.

PERHAPS JESUS WAS TEACHING US THAT AT THE BEGINNING OF HIS LIFE THERE WOULD BE GOOD MIRACLES, BUT THE BEST MIRACLES ARE SAVED FOR THE END!

Maybe He was also teaching us that no matter what we may be like—even stone waterpots of filthy feet water—we can be changed and transformed into something spectacular, something that would surprise people when they encountered us. And maybe most of all,

HE WAS TEACHING US THAT HE IS LORD AND KING OF THE FEAST.

A God of all that is good! The bringer of the best of the best. Following Jesus is meant to be a thrill! FOLLOWING HIM is not about keeping rules, but it IS ABOUT CELEBRATING AND REJOICING IN THE GREAT GOOD that He has to give. It is about living in His kingdom with all the beauty He offers as King. And He doesn't just have a little for us—He has six waterpots of twenty to thirty gallons each. More than enough for anyone and everyone!

ALL OF OUR GREATEST HOPES AND DREAMS WILL EVENTUALLY COME ALIVE AND COME TO PASS IN JESUS CHRIST.

The stories we all hope are true as kids have a fulfillment in part in the story of Jesus. Have you ever noticed that every fairy tale we grow up on has a similar plotline? Everything is fine until a villain or problem comes along to ruin it. AND THEN WE GET A HERO. Someone who goes through a great sacrifice or journey to make everything right again. Why do we love and retell stories like that again and again? It's because they are true! They are the plotline of the greatest story of all time. The story of Jesus Christ. A boy made out of wood who can become real. A peasant girl in rags who becomes a princess. A brutal beast who can be transformed into a kind king. A girl who has been poisoned but can be brought back to life with true love. These stories of change and rescue and love are stories we long for because they are, in part, our story. We all hope for and need a hero who can bring us the kind of good that we usually only find in fairy tales. BUT THE GOOD NEWS IS THAT HIS STORY IS TRUE! It actually happened.

Because of Jesus Christ, there is no death, only life. All goodbyes are only temporary. Because of Jesus Christ, our sins do not have to be our story. We can change and start over. Because of Jesus Christ, we can have hope and faith in a better future.

In this story, when we are broken like Humpty Dumpty by falling off our wall, the king's horses and king's men don't come to put us back together, but the King Himself. He is the giver of all good gifts. He knows exactly what we need, when we need it. We don't have to wish and hope for good things with our fingers crossed—because of Jesus's cross and empty tomb, all things will "work together for good" for those who love Him (Romans 8:28).

Some of you might be wondering whether this is true, because things don't seem to be working out for you. What we have to know is that RiGHT NOW WE LiVE iN THE MiDDLE OF THE STORY. We are still in act two of a three-act play. Not everything is being resolved yet, and THE KiNG HAS NOT TAKEN HiS PLACE ON THE THRONE. But one day He will, and when He comes again we all get our happily ever after! Even though we are experiencing overwhelming amounts of good from Him right now, He is also, as Paul called Him, the "high priest of good things to come" (Hebrews 9:11). There are some blessings and some gifts that we are not experiencing yet. They come at the end.

> Even though He won't reign over the whole world as king until He comes again, we can choose to have Him reign as king of our lives starting today.

We can accept His laws and live the way He governs—by the laws of love and peace. We can love Him and praise Him and honor Him as our Ruler. Isaiah gives us an invitation: "Come ye, and let us go up to the mountain of the Lord, . . . and he will teach us of his ways, and we will walk in his paths" (Isaiah 2:3). The mountain of the Lord is one way of saying the temple. One of the reasons we have the scriptures and the temple is to teach us of His ways. When we make covenants with Him, we are choosing Him to be our king. That might be part of the reason that TEMPLES look so much like castles. They are the HOME OF THE KiNG. The place He invites us to be with Him and become like Him.

One of my favorite Bible stories is about A KING WHO CHOSE JESUS TO BE HIS KING and is found in 2 Samuel chapter 6. Little David, who we talked about fighting Goliath in the last chapter, eventually became the king of Israel. As a king, he led the army in fighting many more battles that the Lord gave him strength to win. The Lord poured out His blessings on David and His people so much that the time period when David ruled was known as the Golden Era of Israel.

When David was anointed as king, one of the first things he wanted to do was take the ark of the covenant to the city of Jerusalem to put it into the tabernacle. The ark of the covenant was a fancy box that Moses and the children of Israel built. It was kept in the Holy of Holies in the ancient temple and represented the holy throne of God. David wanted to give it a permanent place in his city. King David arranged a giant parade and procession in celebration of the ark entering into Jerusalem. This ark represented the Lord and His sacrifice for His people. So as the ark was marched into the city, "DAVID DANCED before the Lord with all his might. . . . David and all the house of Israel brought up the ark of the Lord with shouting, and with the sound of the trumpet" (2 Samuel 6:14–15). Do you love picturing this?? He was not only dancing, but was DANCING WITH ALL OF HIS MIGHT! And you know his dance moves were good! And the trumpets were blowing and they were just praising with all they had. Can I get a witness?? As they walked into the city, David's wife looked out the window and saw the spectacle he was making. Later on that day, she made a comment to him about how silly he looked as the king, dancing before the ark. Kings were supposed to be dignified. More regal. I love David's answer back: "IT WAS BEFORE THE LORD" (v. 21).

DAVID KNEW WHO HIS KING WAS.

HE HAD BEEN CHOSEN BY HIM WHEN HE DIDN'T DESERVE IT. HE HAD BEEN SAVED BY HIM WHEN IT WASN'T EARNED.

His goodness filled his days—all his days. So he was going to dance! And play the trumpets, and clap, and sing, and shout, and let it all burst out of him. "It was before the Lord."

I want to take this approach more often in my life. MORE PRAISING for His goodness. MORE SINGING about His grace. And MORE DANCING because I've been delivered. HE IS WORTH IT. And, oh, can you imagine the celebration when He returns again? I sing the hymn "Come, O Thou King of Kings" in sacrament meeting with a little more volume than the rest. I simply cannot wait!

And neither can so many of my friends. When my friend Nish became a Christian, she was assigned a mentor to help her learn how to follow Jesus Christ. This mentor met with her once a week to show her how to pray, read scripture, and learn to walk in the ways of the Savior. Each Thursday morning when she would drive up to meet her mentor, the front door to her house was always unlocked and there was a standing invitation that she could just walk right in. Every week she would find Nancy, her mentor, in the same spot—by the windows watching the sun rise with anticipation. Then after a moment she would say the same two words: "MAYBE TODAY." Nancy was talking about the Second Coming. She looked forward to it like

Christmas morning. She knew what it meant to have Jesus come and reign as king. A life that is almost too good to be true! I never want to stop being amazed by or anticipating more of His grace. If we are learning about it correctly, it will surprise us around every corner. It will leave us giddy with excitement—like a kid on Christmas Eve. The more we know about Him, the more good we will discover. And the best is yet to come!

We are just barely starting to unwrap all of the gifts He has in store.

He is the wonderful King of all good things now, then, and yet to come.

THE ANTICIPATED KING

Is coming again!
Is the source of all good—past, present, and future.
Will rule and reign with grace and
goodness forever and ever.

⇒ 11 ⇐

CONCLUSION

Have you ever seen a trailer for a movie or had a friend hype up a Netflix show that you got really excited for, and then you went and saw it and it was just blah? Or have you ever dreamt of going some-place in the world and then had the chance and it was not nearly as cool as the pictures made it out to be? Or have you had an item on your bucket list for a long time that you finally got to cross off and it was just . . . okay?

This happened to me in Egypt. I had wanted to go see the pyramids for such a long time. When I was little, I was fascinated by pharaohs and tombs and treasures and mummies, cruising down the Nile and riding through the Sahara. One day I got the chance to go. I was actually going to see the Pyramids of Giza outside of Cairo. I could hardly wait! And then, on the day that I went, I WAS SORT OF UNDERWHELMED. I mean, they were really cool, and I am impressed anyone could have built them, but the experience was just not what I thought it would be. The pyramids were right outside of a super dirty, trashy city, the desert was excru-ciatingly hot, the locals pestered you for money every second, our horse ride got canceled because there are fake companies that take you far out into the desert to rob you or leave you for dead, and the path to get down into the actual pyramids was stuffy, long, and too short for me to stand in. And King Tut? Kind of boring. He was on display in this room that sort of looked like a garage sale of Egyptian artifacts. And the Nile River smelled like the sewer.

I am so happy I went, but it just was not what I had hoped and what it was hyped up to be.

Throughout this book, we have been looking at the different names of Jesus. Names that teach us His attributes and character and what we can expect when we encounter Him. It was written to tell you who He really is. To introduce you to Him. But I want to make you a promise, and this is it:

You will never be disappointed with Him. There is not any way that I could build Him up to be something He isn't. He won't ever be a letdown. It's impossible. He will always be something more. He will knock the socks off your expectations. Jesus is exactly who you always hoped He would be, plus infinity.

In that story of the first Christmas—the first time Jesus came to earth—the story that Dad or Mom reads from the Bible after we open our new jammies—there was an angel who appeared to shepherds out in the Bethlehem fields. I imagine they were a little freaked out. But then the angel reassured them. "Fear not." Don't you worry. "Behold, I bring you good tidings of great joy, which shall be to all people. For unto you is born this day in the city of David a Saviour, which is Christ the Lord" (Luke 2:10–11). The angel came with tidings, or news. Good news!

Did you know the word *gospel* comes from an old English word that actually means "good news"? And WHAT IS THE GOOD NEWS? JESUS. God's greatest gift came to the world, and He was wrapped up in swaddling clothes. "FOR GOD SO LOVED THE WORLD, THAT HE GAVE HiS ONLY BEGOTTEN SON" (John 3:16). The most unobtainable gift of all!

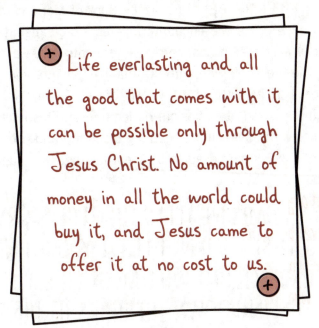

Life everlasting and all the good that comes with it can be possible only through Jesus Christ. No amount of money in all the world could buy it, and Jesus came to offer it at no cost to us.

That is the message we send missionaries with all over the world and the one we tell from pulpits every fast Sunday and around campfires in the summer. It is the best one ever told. It makes the greatest bedtime story and it brings to life every fairy tale ever written.

That is good news! HE iS GOOD NEWS! I have often thought, if someone is preaching about Jesus Christ and it doesn't sound like good news, then I might not be hearing the gospel. The gospel is more than good advice or good manners. Keeping commandments and the "shoulds" and "should nots" are a part of following Him, but they should not dominate our conversations. They are not the best parts. Advice is what you should do; good news is a report of something that has been done. And **WHAT JESUS HAS DONE AND WHAT HE HAS TO GIVE IN THE FUTURE SHOULD IGNITE OUR SOULS AND LEAVE US AMAZED EVERY SINGLE TIME.** Alma, in the Book of Mormon, described an experience of people encountering Jesus's cleansing grace by saying they were "sanctified, and their garments were washed white through the blood of the Lamb" (Alma 13:11). Are you picturing this scene? **WASHED WHITE IN THE BLOOD?** If you dip anything in blood or anything else red, it comes out ruined forever. This image of dipping your favorite shirt into something blood-red and it coming out sparkling white is supposed to be breathtaking. It is supposed to shock you.

WHEN SOMEONE TELLS THE REAL STORY OF JESUS, IT SHOULD NOT LEAVE YOU STANDING ALL AMAZED BUT WILL MOST LIKELY LEAVE YOU FALLING DOWN—PERHAPS AT HIS FEET. I HOPE WE HEAR THIS STORY OFTEN!

When Ammon, a fantastic missionary from the Book of Mormon, got home from his mission, he said to his brother, "Yea, we have reason to praise him forever, for he is the Most High God, and has loosed our brethren from the chains of hell. . . . Therefore, let us glory, yea, **WE WILL GLORY IN THE LORD**; yea, we will rejoice, for our joy is full; yea, we will praise our God forever. Behold, who can glory too much in the Lord? Yea, who can say too much of his great power, and of his mercy, and of his long-suffering towards the children of men? Behold, I say unto you, **I CANNOT SAY THE SMALLEST PART WHICH I FEEL**" (Alma 26:14, 16). Who can say too much? And who can go over the top on rejoicing?

This happens all over scripture. The book of Acts in the New Testament is a collection of stories of the Apostles preaching and teaching about Jesus after His Resurrection and return to heaven. In one of these stories, which you can read in Acts chapter 3, two of the disciples, Peter and John, are together at the temple heading into a gate called "beautiful" when they notice a man sitting on the stone steps begging for money (see Acts 3:1–11). It was a man who was there every day. Every morning, someone would carry him to his little spot right outside the gate of the temple to beg. He had no other way of working or earning money since he was born unable to walk. His parents never got the thrill of seeing him take his first steps. He'd never played Little League baseball or been asked to a school dance. While everyone else went off to college and was offered big salaries and new jobs, all he got were judgmental glares and a few coins dropped into his bowl. What dreams did he dream? What did he wish his life could have been like? What hopes slowly disappeared over time? For years, he sat on the same steps, his head down and his hands out to everyone and anyone who passed by. When the two disciples came near him, he asked them for any pocket change they could spare. Peter stopped, looked down at the man, and said, "Look on us." Now looking at him in his eyes, Peter said to the crippled man,

"Silver and gold have I none; but such as I have give I thee: In the name of Jesus Christ of Nazareth rise up and walk" (Acts 3:6).

He then reached down and grabbed the man by the right hand and lifted him to his feet. Feet that now worked! "And he leaping up stood, and walked, and entered with them into the temple, walking, and leaping, and praising God" (v. 8).

The man had come to that temple every day for as long as he could remember. For years he had watched others pass by and gather together in that holy place for prayer while he sat outside alone.

He was helpless and hopeless— until he heard the name of Jesus.

That day the man was healed in the name of Jesus Christ, and his whole world turned right-side up. I love picturing him standing, taking his first steps, and then leaping around the temple grounds in praise of God. Oh, he made a scene! Like David dancing before the Lord! Can you picture him just laughing and twirling as he looked back and forth at Peter and then his feet and then Peter and his feet again? He spoke no words—just praises. He could walk! He could run! He could jump! He could live! And now he could enter the holy gates. All because of Jesus.

PEOPLE ARE NEVER THE SAME AFTER THEY HAVE AN AUTHENTIC RUN-IN WITH JESUS CHRIST. It moves people from lame to leaping. They climb trees and walk through oceans and start life again. Do you remember when Jesus surprised Nathanael by recognizing him under the fig tree? On that day He promised him, "Thou shalt see greater things than these" (John 1:50). LIFE FOLLOWING JESUS IS ALWAYS FILLED WITH THOSE GREATER THINGS.

You might feel like the man on the steps—waiting or begging or hoping for something. Or maybe just feeling a little bit lame in life. Whatever it is that you may be seeking for, you can find it in Him.

He is the Mighty Jehovah and can do breathtaking miracles.

He is the Watchful Shepherd and will watch over and care for you.

HE IS THE LIGHT OF THE WORLD AND CAN FILL YOUR HEART WITH HOPE.

HE IS THE EVER-PRESENT EMMANUEL
AND WILL BE WITH YOU IN YOUR STORY.

He is the Tender Jesus and will meet you with gentleness.

He is the Hope of Israel and is quick to forgive.

He is the Unfailing Deliverer and will never leave you helpless.

HE IS THE LAMB OF GOD WHO LAID DOWN HIS LIFE FOR YOU.

He is your Loyal Advocate and will speak up for you,
fight for you, and defend you.

And He is the Anticipated King who will bring all good things.
Or we may even say, "the greater things."

HE IS WHO HE WILL ALWAYS BE:
A REDEEMER WHO WILL
SAVE YOU BY ANY MEANS.

WHO DO YOU NEED HIM
TO BE TODAY?

Each Sunday we hear a prayer in church over the sacrament that includes a covenant and promise to take upon us His name. I love the emphasis on and reminder of His name. A while ago, during a typical Monday-morning chat with my friend Daisy—remember him?—he asked me a question that has taken this to a next-level experience for me. He mentioned that line in the sacrament prayer, the one about Jesus's name, and then asked me, "BUT WHICH NAME?" He said that on a recent Sunday as he sat in his seat while the sacrament was blessed, he heard that phrase and started thinking of all the different names of Jesus that he could.

The Advocate. The Lamb. The Shepherd. The Messiah. What did each of those names mean to him? What did they teach about who He was and the kind of life He lived?

Daisy chose one and thought—How had Jesus filled that particular role for him that past week? Did He deliver him? Rescue him? Defend him? Don't you love the idea of thinking about that each Sunday during the sacrament? WHAT ARE HIS NAMES, AND HOW HAS HE BEEN THAT FOR ME?

And like thinking often does, it led my friend to another question.

"THIS WEEK, HOW CAN I TAKE THAT NAME OF JESUS UPON ME AND BE THAT FOR SOMEONE ELSE?"

How can I defend, rescue, and love like He did? It is a life pattern I quickly joined him on. A pattern to choose a name that teaches His character, watch and remember how He is that name for me, and then try to live that same way, as His disciple, to others. I am becoming more aware of His stunning character and His presence in my story, and it is making me want to be more like Him. This pattern has been changing me.

For a long, long time, we did not have a picture or painting of Jesus in our home. Don't judge me. The problem is I am just an art snob. I couldn't find one that spoke to me, and I didn't want the same one everyone else had. Christmas after Christmas and birthday after birthday, Jenny would give me a coupon to go pick out my favorite picture of Jesus as my gift. But I never could. (And she never gave me another gift—so she kind of owes me!) One year, I took the challenge to study the life and names of Jesus Christ. I read about Him, thought about Him, taught about Him, and tried with my whole heart to live like Him. It was one of my favorite times of my life. As the year was wrapping up, I went to Costco to eat some samples and spend a million dollars on groceries. At the Costco by our house, every Christmas a little shop is set up near the checkout stand with paintings of temples and of Christ. As I pushed my overly filled cart up to the display, A PICTURE OF THE SAVIOR CAUGHT MY EYE. I moved closer and stared at it in wonder. My heart jumped. It moved me to tears. How had I never seen this one? It was breathtaking. This was the one! As I moved down the row of paintings, I stopped at each one and had the same reaction. Where had this artist been all my life?! He was incredible. Then I had a realization. Those paintings had been there for years. They had never changed, and there was nothing new. *I* had changed, and my feelings for Jesus had become new. THE PAINTING WASN'T THE INCREDIBLE THING—JESUS WAS. I had started to adore Him and love Him in a way I never had before. He became "my Jesus."

We got started together, you and me, on this journey of learning about Jesus and beginning a lifelong friendship, but let's make a deal right now that we keep it up. Let's continue to study who He is and then look for Him in our life once we set this book down. Let's watch for the same God we see in the scriptures coming off of the pages and coming alive in our story. And then let's talk about Him more and try to live like Him.

HE IS THE WAY. IT'S ANOTHER ONE OF HIS NAMES.
HE IS THE WAY TO EVERY GIFT AND THRILL.
THE WAY TO HAPPINESS AND HOPE, FORGIVENESS AND
FULFILLMENT, LEAPING AND LIFE EVERLASTING.

His names teach us who He is. They teach us what He can be and hopes to be to all of us.

So "seek this Jesus of whom the prophets and apostles have written" (Ether 12:41).

And as you seek Him diligently, maybe one day you will be standing in line at Disneyland, munching on one of those fancy churros, and you will overhear a name that causes your heart to leap. The name of Jesus. Your Jesus. You will hear it and realize that He has become near and dear and irresistible to your heart. The same way you already are to His.

NOTES

1. See 1 Nephi 8:10–11, Alma 32:42.
2. John R. Lasater, "Shepherds in Israel," *Ensign*, May 1988.
3. Ronald A. Rasband, "Jesus Christ Is the Answer," February 8, 2019.
4. See Henry B. Eyring, "O Remember, Remember," *Ensign*, November 2007.
5. Bible Dictionary, "Joshua."
6. Luke 15:1–2, The Message.
7. Ezra Taft Benson, "Keeping the Law of Chastity," *Teachings of Presidents of the Church: Ezra Taft Benson* (2014), 217–28.
8. Boyd K. Packer, "The Plan of Happiness," *Ensign*, May 2015.
9. See J. E. Stambaugh and D.L. Balch, *The Social World of the First Christians*, (SPCK, 1986).
10. Boyd K. Packer, "Atonement, Agency, Accountability," *Ensign*, May 1988.
11. Neal A. Maxwell, *The Promise of Discipleship* (Salt Lake City: Deseret Book, 2010), 80–84.
12. See, for example, John W. Welch, "The Good Samaritan," *Ensign*, February 2007.
13. Parable loosely adapted from a story told in Thomas B. Griffith, "The Root of Christian Doctrine," *Ensign*, August 2007.
14. See Revelation 12:1–10
15. See Russell M. Nelson, "Jesus Christ—Our Master and More," Brigham Young University fireside, February 2, 1992, 4; speeches.byu.edu.
16. See 1 John 2:1, footnote.
17. See https://www.nps.gov/valr/learn/historyculture/brothersassignedarizona.htm.
18. In *History of the Church*, 5:360–61; punctuation modernized; from a discourse given by Joseph Smith on April 16, 1843, in Nauvoo, Illinois; reported by Wilford Woodruff and Willard Richards.
19. Andrew J. Workman, in "Recollections of the Prophet Joseph Smith," *Juvenile Instructor*, October 15, 1892, 641.

ABOUT THE AUTHOR

DAVID BUTLER is by day a religious educator sharing his fierce love for the scriptures with anyone willing to listen. By night he is a fort builder, waffle maker, sports coach, and storyteller for his six darling kids. Somewhere in between, he is a motivational speaker and writer. He loves, loves, loves good food, spontaneous adventures, Christmas morning, the first day of summer, and every other day of summer. Above all he loves people. He has chosen as his life motto, "Stuff no mattah. People mattah." He and his adorable wife, Jenny, live with their family amid the snowcapped peaks of the Mountain West, but they often dream of a beach house on a sunny shore somewhere.

 @mrdavebutler